Types & Grammar

Kyle Simpson

Beijing · Cambridge · Farnham · Köln · Sebastopol · Tokyo

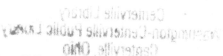

You Don't Know JS: Types & Grammar

by Kyle Simpson

Printed in the United States of America.

Published by O'Reilly Media, Inc., 1005 Gravenstein Highway North, Sebastopol, CA 95472.

O'Reilly books may be purchased for educational, business, or sales promotional use. Online editions are also available for most titles (*http://safaribooksonline.com*). For more information, contact our corporate/institutional sales department: 800-998-9938 or *corporate@oreilly.com*.

Editors: Simon St. Laurent and Brian MacDonald
Production Editor: Kristen Brown
Copyeditor: Christina Edwards

Proofreader: Charles Roumeliotis
Interior Designer: David Futato
Cover Designer: Ellie Volckhausen

February 2015:   First Edition

Revision History for the First Edition

2015-01-23:   First Release

See *http://oreilly.com/catalog/errata.csp?isbn=9781491904190* for release details.

978-1-491-90419-0

[LSI]

Table of Contents

Foreword

It was once said, "JavaScript is the only language developers don't learn to use before using it."

I laugh each time I hear that quote because it was true for me and I suspect it was for many other developers. JavaScript, and maybe even CSS and HTML, were not among the core computer science languages taught at college in the Internet's early days, so personal development was very much based on the budding developer's search and "view source" abilities to piece together these basic web languages.

I still remember my first high school website project. The task was to create any type of web store, and me being a James Bond fan, I decided to create a Goldeneye store. It had everything: the Goldeneye MIDI theme song playing in the background, JavaScript-powered crosshairs following the mouse around the screen, and a gunshot sound that played upon every click. Q would have been proud of this masterpiece of a website.

I tell that story because I did back then what many developers are doing today: I copied-and-pasted chunks of JavaScript code into my project without having a clue about what's actually happening. The widespread use of JavaScript toolkits like jQuery have, in their own small way, perpetuated this pattern of not learning of core JavaScript.

I'm not disparaging JavaScript toolkit use; after all, I'm a member of the MooTools JavaScript team! But the reason JavaScript toolkits are as powerful as they are is because their developers know the fundamentals, and their "gotchas," and apply them magnificently. As useful as these toolkits are, it's still incredibly important to know the basics of the language, and with books like Kyle Simpson's *You Don't Know JS* series, there's no excuse not to learn them.

Types & Grammar, the third installment of the series, is an excellent look at the core JavaScript fundamentals that copy-and-paste and JavaScript toolkits don't and could never teach you. Coercion and its pitfalls, natives as constructors, and the whole gamut of JavaScript basics are thoroughly explained with focused code examples. Like the other books in this series, Kyle cuts straight to the point, with no fluff and wordsmithing—exactly the type of tech book I love.

Enjoy *Types & Grammar* and don't let it get too far away from your desk!

—*David Walsh (http://davidwalsh.name),*
Senior Web Developer at Mozilla

Preface

I'm sure you noticed, but "JS" in the series title is not an abbreviation for words used to curse about JavaScript, though cursing at the language's quirks is something we can probably all identify with!

From the earliest days of the Web, JavaScript has been a foundational technology that drives interactive experience around the content we consume. While flickering mouse trails and annoying pop-up prompts may be where JavaScript started, nearly two decades later, the technology and capability of JavaScript has grown many orders of magnitude, and few doubt its importance at the heart of the world's most widely available software platform: the Web.

But as a language, it has perpetually been a target for a great deal of criticism, owing partly to its heritage but even more to its design philosophy. Even the name evokes, as Brendan Eich once put it, "dumb kid brother" status next to its more mature older brother Java. But the name is merely an accident of politics and marketing. The two languages are vastly different in many important ways. "JavaScript" is as related to "Java" as "Carnival" is to "Car."

Because JavaScript borrows concepts and syntax idioms from several languages, including proud C-style procedural roots as well as subtle, less obvious Scheme/Lisp-style functional roots, it is exceedingly approachable to a broad audience of developers, even those with little to no programming experience. The "Hello World" of JavaScript is so simple that the language is inviting and easy to get comfortable with in early exposure.

While JavaScript is perhaps one of the easiest languages to get up and running with, its eccentricities make solid mastery of the language a vastly less common occurrence than in many other languages. Where it takes a pretty in-depth knowledge of a language like C or C++ to write a full-scale program, full-scale production JavaScript can, and often does, barely scratch the surface of what the language can do.

Sophisticated concepts that are deeply rooted into the language tend instead to surface themselves in *seemingly* simplistic ways, such as passing around functions as callbacks, which encourages the JavaScript developer to just use the language as-is and not worry too much about what's going on under the hood.

It is simultaneously a simple, easy-to-use language that has broad appeal, and a complex and nuanced collection of language mechanics that without careful study will elude *true understanding* even for the most seasoned of JavaScript developers.

Therein lies the paradox of JavaScript, the Achilles' heel of the language, the challenge we are presently addressing. Because JavaScript *can* be used without understanding, the understanding of the language is often never attained.

Mission

If at every point that you encounter a surprise or frustration in JavaScript, your response is to add it to the blacklist (as some are accustomed to doing), you soon will be relegated to a hollow shell of the richness of JavaScript.

While this subset has been famously dubbed "The Good Parts," I would implore you, dear reader, to instead consider it the "The Easy Parts," "The Safe Parts," or even "The Incomplete Parts."

This *You Don't Know JS* series offers a contrary challenge: learn and deeply understand *all* of JavaScript, even and especially "The Tough Parts."

Here, we address head-on the tendency of JS developers to learn "just enough" to get by, without ever forcing themselves to learn exactly how and why the language behaves the way it does. Furthermore, we eschew the common advice to retreat when the road gets rough.

I am not content, nor should you be, at stopping once something just works and not really knowing *why*. I gently challenge you to journey down that bumpy "road less traveled" and embrace all that

JavaScript is and can do. With that knowledge, no technique, no framework, no popular buzzword acronym of the week will be beyond your understanding.

These books each take on specific core parts of the language that are most commonly misunderstood or under-understood, and dive very deep and exhaustively into them. You should come away from reading with a firm confidence in your understanding, not just of the theoretical, but the practical "what you need to know" bits.

The JavaScript you know right now is probably parts handed down to you by others who've been burned by incomplete understanding. *That* JavaScript is but a shadow of the true language. You don't really know JavaScript, *yet*, but if you dig into this series, you will. Read on, my friends. JavaScript awaits you.

Review

JavaScript is awesome. It's easy to learn partially, and much harder to learn completely (or even *sufficiently*). When developers encounter confusion, they usually blame the language instead of their lack of understanding. These books aim to fix that, inspiring a strong appreciation for the language you can now, and *should*, deeply know.

 Many of the examples in this book assume modern (and future-reaching) JavaScript engine environments, such as ES6. Some code may not work as described if run in older (pre-ES6) engines.

Conventions Used in This Book

The following typographical conventions are used in this book:

Italic
: Indicates new terms, URLs, email addresses, filenames, and file extensions.

`Constant width`
: Used for program listings, as well as within paragraphs to refer to program elements such as variable or function names, databases, data types, environment variables, statements, and keywords.

Constant width bold

Shows commands or other text that should be typed literally by the user.

Constant width italic

Shows text that should be replaced with user-supplied values or by values determined by context.

This element signifies a tip or suggestion.

This element signifies a general note.

This element indicates a warning or caution.

Using Code Examples

Supplemental material (code examples, exercises, etc.) is available for download at *http://bit.ly/ydkjs-types-code*.

This book is here to help you get your job done. In general, if example code is offered with this book, you may use it in your programs and documentation. You do not need to contact us for permission unless you're reproducing a significant portion of the code. For example, writing a program that uses several chunks of code from this book does not require permission. Selling or distributing a CD-ROM of examples from O'Reilly books does require permission. Answering a question by citing this book and quoting example code does not require permission. Incorporating a significant amount of example code from this book into your product's documentation does require permission.

We appreciate, but do not require, attribution. An attribution usually includes the title, author, publisher, and ISBN. For example: "*You Don't Know JavaScript: Types & Grammar* by Kyle Simpson (O'Reilly). Copyright 2015 Getify Solutions, Inc., 978-1-491-90419-0."

If you feel your use of code examples falls outside fair use or the permission given above, feel free to contact us at *permissions@oreilly.com*.

Safari® Books Online

 *Safari Books Online* is an on-demand digital library that delivers expert content in both book and video form from the world's leading authors in technology and business.

Technology professionals, software developers, web designers, and business and creative professionals use Safari Books Online as their primary resource for research, problem solving, learning, and certification training.

Safari Books Online offers a range of plans and pricing for enterprise, government, education, and individuals.

Members have access to thousands of books, training videos, and prepublication manuscripts in one fully searchable database from publishers like O'Reilly Media, Prentice Hall Professional, Addison-Wesley Professional, Microsoft Press, Sams, Que, Peachpit Press, Focal Press, Cisco Press, John Wiley & Sons, Syngress, Morgan Kaufmann, IBM Redbooks, Packt, Adobe Press, FT Press, Apress, Manning, New Riders, McGraw-Hill, Jones & Bartlett, Course Technology, and hundreds more. For more information about Safari Books Online, please visit us online.

How to Contact Us

Please address comments and questions concerning this book to the publisher:

O'Reilly Media, Inc.
1005 Gravenstein Highway North
Sebastopol, CA 95472
800-998-9938 (in the United States or Canada)
707-829-0515 (international or local)
707-829-0104 (fax)

We have a web page for this book, where we list errata, examples, and any additional information. You can access this page at *http://bit.ly/ydkjs_types-and-grammar*.

To comment or ask technical questions about this book, send email to *bookquestions@oreilly.com*.

For more information about our books, courses, conferences, and news, see our website at *http://www.oreilly.com*.

Find us on Facebook: *http://facebook.com/oreilly*

Follow us on Twitter: *http://twitter.com/oreillymedia*

Watch us on YouTube: *http://www.youtube.com/oreillymedia*

CHAPTER 1

Types

Most developers would say that a dynamic language (like JS) does not have *types*. Let's see what the ES5.1 specification (*http://www.ecma-international.org/ecma-262/5.1/*) has to say on the topic:

> Algorithms within this specification manipulate values each of which has an associated type. The possible value types are exactly those defined in this clause. Types are further sub-classified into ECMAScript language types and specification types.

> An ECMAScript language type corresponds to values that are directly manipulated by an ECMAScript programmer using the ECMAScript language. The ECMAScript language types are Undefined, Null, Boolean, String, Number, and Object.

Now, if you're a fan of strongly typed (statically typed) languages, you may object to this usage of the word "type." In those languages, "type" means a whole lot *more* than it does here in JS.

Some people say JS shouldn't claim to have "types," and they should instead be called "tags" or perhaps "subtypes."

Bah! We're going to use this rough definition (the same one that seems to drive the wording of the spec): a *type* is an intrinsic, built-in set of characteristics that uniquely identifies the behavior of a particular value and distinguishes it from other values, both to the engine *and* to the developer.

In other words, if both the engine and the developer treat value 42 (the number) differently than they treat value "42" (the string), then those two values have different *types*—number and string, respectively. When you use 42, you are *intending* to do something numeric, like math. But when you use "42", you are *intending* to do something string'ish, like outputting to the page, etc. These two values have different types.

That's by no means a perfect definition. But it's good enough for this discussion. And it's consistent with how JS describes itself.

A Type by Any Other Name...

Beyond academic definition disagreements, why does it matter if JavaScript has *types* or not?

Having a proper understanding of each *type* and its intrinsic behavior is absolutely essential to understanding how to properly and accurately convert values to different types (see Chapter 4). Nearly every JS program ever written will need to handle value coercion in some shape or form, so it's important you do so responsibly and with confidence.

If you have the number value 42, but you want to treat it like a string, such as pulling out the "2" as a character in position 1, you obviously must first convert (coerce) the value from number to string.

That seems simple enough.

But there are many different ways that such coercion can happen. Some of these ways are explicit, easy to reason about, and reliable. But if you're not careful, coercion can happen in very strange and surprising ways.

Coercion confusion is perhaps one of the most profound frustrations for JavaScript developers. It has often been criticized as being so *dangerous* as to be considered a flaw in the design of the language, to be shunned and avoided.

Armed with a full understanding of JavaScript types, we're aiming to illustrate why coercion's *bad reputation* is largely overhyped and somewhat undeserved—to flip your perspective so you see coercion's power and usefulness. But first, we have to get a much better grip on values and types.

Built-in Types

JavaScript defines seven built-in types:

- `null`
- `undefined`
- `boolean`
- `number`
- `string`
- `object`
- `symbol`—added in ES6!

 All of these types except `object` are called "primitives."

The `typeof` operator inspects the type of the given value, and always returns one of seven string values—surprisingly, there's not an exact 1-to-1 match with the seven built-in types we just listed:

```
typeof undefined     === "undefined"; // true
typeof true          === "boolean";   // true
typeof 42            === "number";    // true
typeof "42"          === "string";    // true
typeof { life: 42 }  === "object";    // true

// added in ES6!
typeof Symbol()      === "symbol";    // true
```

These six listed types have values of the corresponding type and return a string value of the same name, as shown. `Symbol` is a new data type as of ES6, and will be covered in Chapter 3.

As you may have noticed, I excluded `null` from the above listing. It's *special*—special in the sense that it's buggy when combined with the `typeof` operator:

```
typeof null === "object"; // true
```

It would have been nice (and correct!) if it returned `"null"`, but this original bug in JS has persisted for nearly two decades, and will likely never be fixed because there's so much existing web content that relies on its buggy behavior that "fixing" the bug would *create* more "bugs" and break a lot of web software.

If you want to test for a null value using its type, you need a compound condition:

```
var a = null;

(!a && typeof a === "object"); // true
```

null is the only primitive value that is "falsy" (aka false-like; see Chapter 4) but which also returns "object" from the typeof check.

So what's the seventh string value that typeof can return?

```
typeof function a(){ /* .. */ } === "function"; // true
```

It's easy to think that function would be a top-level built-in type in JS, especially given this behavior of the typeof operator. However, if you read the spec, you'll see it's actually somewhat of a "subtype" of object. Specifically, a function is referred to as a "callable object"— an object that has an internal [[Call]] property that allows it to be invoked.

The fact that functions are actually objects is quite useful. Most importantly, they can have properties. For example:

```
function a(b,c) {
    /* .. */
}
```

The function object has a length property set to the number of formal parameters it is declared with:

```
a.length; // 2
```

Since you declared the function with two formal named parameters (b and c), the "length of the function" is 2.

What about arrays? They're native to JS, so are they a special type?

```
typeof [1,2,3] === "object"; // true
```

Nope, just objects. It's most appropriate to think of them also as a "subtype" of object (see Chapter 3), in this case with the additional characteristics of being numerically indexed (as opposed to just being string-keyed like plain objects) and maintaining an automatically updated .length property.

Values as Types

In JavaScript, variables don't have types—*values have types*. Variables can hold any value, at any time.

Another way to think about JS types is that JS doesn't have "type enforcement," in that the engine doesn't insist that a *variable* always holds values of the *same initial type* that it starts out with. A variable can, in one assignment statement, hold a string, and in the next hold a number, and so on.

The *value* 42 has an intrinsic type of number, and its *type* cannot be changed. Another value, like "42" with the string type, can be created *from* the number value 42 through a process called *coercion* (see Chapter 4).

If you use typeof against a variable, it's not asking "What's the type of the variable?" as it may seem, since JS variables have no types. Instead, it's asking "What's the type of the value *in* the variable?"

```
var a = 42;
typeof a; // "number"

a = true;
typeof a; // "boolean"
```

The typeof operator always returns a string. So:

```
typeof typeof 42; // "string"
```

The first typeof 42 returns "number", and typeof "number" is "string".

undefined Versus "undeclared"

Variables that have no value *currently* actually have the undefined value. Calling typeof against such variables will return "undefined":

```
var a;

typeof a; // "undefined"

var b = 42;
var c;

// later
b = c;
```

```
typeof b; // "undefined"
typeof c; // "undefined"
```

It's tempting for most developers to think of the word "undefined" as a synonym for "undeclared." However, in JS, these two concepts are quite different.

An "undefined" variable is one that has been declared in the accessible scope, but *at the moment* has no other value in it. By contrast, an "undeclared" variable is one that has not been formally declared in the accessible scope.

Consider:

```
var a;

a; // undefined
b; // ReferenceError: b is not defined
```

An annoying confusion is the error message that browsers assign to this condition. As you can see, the message is "b is not defined," which is of course very easy and reasonable to confuse with "b is undefined." Yet again, "undefined" and "is not defined" are very different things. It'd be nice if the browsers said something like "b is not found" or "b is not declared" to reduce the confusion!

There's also a special behavior associated with typeof as it relates to undeclared variables that even further reinforces the confusion. Consider:

```
var a;

typeof a; // "undefined"

typeof b; // "undefined"
```

The typeof operator returns "undefined" even for "undeclared" (or "not defined") variables. Notice that there was no error thrown when we executed typeof b, even though b is an undeclared variable. This is a special safety guard in the behavior of typeof.

Similar to above, it would have been nice if typeof used with an undeclared variable returned "undeclared" instead of conflating the result value with the different "undefined" case.

typeof Undeclared

Nevertheless, this safety guard is a useful feature when dealing with JavaScript in the browser, where multiple script files can load variables into the shared global namespace.

 Many developers believe there should never be any variables in the global namespace, and that everything should be contained in modules and private/separate namespaces. This is great in theory but nearly impossible in practice; still, it's a good goal to strive toward! Fortunately, ES6 added first-class support for modules, which will eventually make that much more practical.

As a simple example, imagine having a "debug mode" in your program that is controlled by a global variable (flag) called DEBUG. You'd want to check if that variable was declared before performing a debug task like logging a message to the console. A top-level global var DEBUG = true declaration would only be included in a "debug.js" file, which you only load into the browser when you're in development/testing, but not in production.

However, you have to take care in how you check for the global DEBUG variable in the rest of your application code, so that you don't throw a ReferenceError. The safety guard on typeof is our friend in this case:

```
// oops, this would throw an error!
if (DEBUG) {
    console.log( "Debugging is starting" );
}

// this is a safe existence check
if (typeof DEBUG !== "undefined") {
    console.log( "Debugging is starting" );
}
```

This sort of check is useful even if you're not dealing with user-defined variables (like DEBUG). If you are doing a feature check for a built-in API, you may also find it helpful to check without throwing an error:

```
if (typeof atob === "undefined") {
    atob = function() { /*..*/ };
}
```

If you're defining a "polyfill" for a feature if it doesn't already exist, you probably want to avoid using `var` to make the `atob` declaration. If you declare `var atob` inside the `if` statement, this declaration is hoisted (see the *Scope & Closures* title in this series) to the top of the scope, even if the `if` condition doesn't pass (because the global `atob` already exists!). In some browsers and for some special types of global built-in variables (often called "host objects"), this duplicate declaration may throw an error. Omitting the `var` prevents this hoisted declaration.

Another way of doing these checks against global variables but without the safety guard feature of `typeof` is to observe that all global variables are also properties of the global object, which in the browser is basically the `window` object. So, the above checks could have been done (quite safely) as:

```
if (window.DEBUG) {
    // ..
}

if (!window.atob) {
    // ..
}
```

Unlike referencing undeclared variables, there is no `ReferenceError` thrown if you try to access an object property (even on the global `window` object) that doesn't exist.

On the other hand, manually referencing the global variable with a `window` reference is something some developers prefer to avoid, especially if your code needs to run in multiple JS environments (not just browsers, but server-side node.js, for instance), where the global variable may not always be called `window`.

Technically, this safety guard on `typeof` is useful even if you're not using global variables, though these circumstances are less common, and some developers may find this design approach less desirable. Imagine a utility function that you want others to copy-and-paste into their programs or modules, in which you want to check to see if the including program has defined a certain variable (so that you can use it) or not:

```
function doSomethingCool() {
    var helper =
        (typeof FeatureXYZ !== "undefined") ?
        FeatureXYZ :
        function() { /*.. default feature ..*/ };

    var val = helper();
    // ..
}
```

doSomethingCool() tests for a variable called FeatureXYZ, and if found, uses it, but if not, uses its own. Now, if someone includes this utility into their module/program, it safely checks if they've defined FeatureXYZ or not:

```
// an IIFE (see the "Immediately Invoked Function Expressions"
// discussion in the Scope & Closures title in this series)
(function(){
    function FeatureXYZ() { /*.. my XYZ feature ..*/ }

    // include `doSomethingCool(..)`
    function doSomethingCool() {
        var helper =
            (typeof FeatureXYZ !== "undefined") ?
            FeatureXYZ :
            function() { /*.. default feature ..*/ };

        var val = helper();
        // ..
    }

    doSomethingCool();
})();
```

Here, FeatureXYZ is not at all a global variable, but we're still using the safety guard of typeof to make it safe to check for. And importantly, here there is *no* object we can use (like we did for global variables with window.___) to make the check, so typeof is quite helpful.

Other developers would prefer a design pattern called "dependency injection," where instead of doSomethingCool() inspecting implicitly for FeatureXYZ to be defined outside/around it, it would need to have the dependency explicitly passed in, like:

```
function doSomethingCool(FeatureXYZ) {
    var helper = FeatureXYZ ||
        function() { /*.. default feature ..*/ };

    var val = helper();
```

```
        // ..
    }
```

There's lots of options when designing such functionality. No one pattern here is "correct" or "wrong"—there are various trade-offs to each approach. But overall, it's nice that the `typeof` undeclared safety guard gives us more options.

Review

JavaScript has seven built-in *types*: `null`, `undefined`, `boolean`, `number`, `string`, `object`, and `symbol`. They can be identified by the `typeof` operator.

Variables don't have types, but the values in them do. These types define the intrinsic behavior of the values.

Many developers will assume "undefined" and "undeclared" are roughly the same thing, but in JavaScript, they're quite different. `undefined` is a value that a declared variable can hold. "Undeclared" means a variable has never been declared.

JavaScript unfortunately kind of conflates these two terms, not only in its error messages ("ReferenceError: a is not defined") but also in the return values of `typeof`, which is `"undefined"` for both cases.

However, the safety guard (preventing an error) on `typeof` when used against an undeclared variable can be helpful in certain cases.

CHAPTER 2

Values

arrays, strings, and numbers are the most basic building blocks of any program, but JavaScript has some unique characteristics with these types that may either delight or confound you.

Let's look at several of the built-in value types in JS, and explore how we can more fully understand and correctly leverage their behaviors.

Arrays

As compared to other type-enforced languages, JavaScript arrays are just containers for any type of value, from string to number to object to even another array (which is how you get multidimensional arrays):

```
var a = [ 1, "2", [3] ];

a.length;        // 3
a[0] === 1;      // true
a[2][0] === 3;   // true
```

You don't need to presize your arrays (see "Array(..)" on page 44), you can just declare them and add values as you see fit:

```
var a = [ ];

a.length;    // 0

a[0] = 1;
a[1] = "2";
a[2] = [ 3 ];

a.length;    // 3
```

 Using `delete` on an `array` value will remove that slot from the `array`, but even if you remove the final element, it does not update the `length` property, so be careful! We'll cover the `delete` operator itself in more detail in Chapter 5.

Be careful about creating "sparse" `arrays` (leaving or creating empty/ missing slots):

```
var a = [ ];

a[0] = 1;
// no `a[1]` slot set here
a[2] = [ 3 ];

a[1];        // undefined

a.length;    // 3
```

While that works, it can lead to some confusing behavior with the "empty slots" you leave in between. While the slot appears to have the `undefined` value in it, it will not behave the same as if the slot is explicitly set (`a[1] = undefined`). See "Array(..)" on page 44 for more information.

`arrays` are numerically indexed (as you'd expect), but the tricky thing is that they also are objects that can have `string` keys/properties added to them (but which don't count toward the `length` of the array):

```
var a = [ ];

a[0] = 1;
a["foobar"] = 2;

a.length;        // 1
a["foobar"];     // 2
a.foobar;        // 2
```

However, a gotcha to be aware of is that if a string value intended as a key can be coerced to a standard base-10 number, then it is assumed that you wanted to use it as a number index rather than as a string key!

```
var a = [ ];

a["13"] = 42;

a.length; // 14
```

Generally, it's not a great idea to add string keys/properties to arrays. Use objects for holding values in keys/properties, and save arrays for strictly numerically indexed values.

Array-Likes

There will be occasions where you need to convert an array-like value (a numerically indexed collection of values) into a true array, usually so you can call array utilities (like indexOf(..), concat(..), forEach(..), etc.) against the collection of values.

For example, various DOM query operations return lists of DOM elements that are not true arrays but are array-like enough for our conversion purposes. Another common example is when functions expose the arguments (array-like) object (as of ES6, deprecated) to access the arguments as a list.

One very common way to make such a conversion is to borrow the slice(..) utility against the value:

```
function foo() {
    var arr = Array.prototype.slice.call( arguments );
    arr.push( "bam" );
    console.log( arr );
}

foo( "bar", "baz" ); // ["bar","baz","bam"]
```

If slice() is called without any other parameters, as it effectively is in the above snippet, the default values for its parameters have the effect of duplicating the array (or, in this case, array-like).

As of ES6, there's also a built-in utility called Array.from(..) that can do the same task:

```
...
var arr = Array.from( arguments );
...
```

 Array.from(..) has several powerful capabilities, and will be covered in detail in the *ES6 & Beyond* title in this series.

Strings

It's a very common belief that `strings` are essentially just `arrays` of characters. While the implementation under the covers may or may not use `arrays`, it's important to realize that JavaScript `strings` are really not the same as `arrays` of characters. The similarity is mostly just skin-deep.

For example, let's consider these two values:

```
var a = "foo";
var b = ["f","o","o"];
```

Strings do have a shallow resemblance to `arrays`—they are array-likes, as above. For instance, both of them have a `length` property, an `indexOf(..)` method (array version only as of ES5), and a `con cat(..)` method:

```
[source,js]

a.length;                           // 3
b.length;                           // 3

a.indexOf( "o" );                   // 1
b.indexOf( "o" );                   // 1

var c = a.concat( "bar" );          // "foobar"
var d = b.concat( ["b","a","r"] );  // ["f","o","o","b","a","r"]

a === c;                            // false
b === d;                            // false

a;                                 // "foo"
b;                                 // ["f","o","o"]
```

So, they're both basically just "arrays of characters," right? Not exactly:

```
a[1] = "O";
b[1] = "O";

a;  // "foo"
b;  // ["f","O","o"]
```

JavaScript `strings` are immutable, while `arrays` are quite mutable.
Moreover, the a[1] character position access form was not always
widely valid JavaScript. Older versions of IE did not allow that syntax (but now they do). Instead, the *correct* approach has been
a.charAt(1).

A further consequence of immutable `strings` is that none of the
`string` methods that alter its contents can modify in-place, but
rather must create and return new `strings`. By contrast, many of the
`array` methods that change array contents actually *do* modify in-
place:

```
c = a.toUpperCase();
a === c;    // false
a;          // "foo"
c;          // "FOO"

b.push( "!" );
b;          // ["f","O","o","!"]
```

Also, many of the `array` methods that could be helpful when dealing
with `strings` are not actually available for them, but we can "borrow" nonmutation `array` methods against our `string`:

```
a.join;     // undefined
a.map;      // undefined

var c = Array.prototype.join.call( a, "-" );
var d = Array.prototype.map.call( a, function(v){
    return v.toUpperCase() + ".";
} ).join( "" );

c;          // "f-o-o"
d;          // "F.O.O."
```

Let's take another example: reversing a `string` (incidentally, a common JavaScript interview trivia question!). `arrays` have a reverse()
in-place mutator method, but `strings` do not:

```
a.reverse;      // undefined

b.reverse();    // ["!","o","O","f"]
b;              // ["!","o","O","f"]
```

Unfortunately, this "borrowing" doesn't work with `array` mutators, because `strings` are immutable and thus can't be modified in place:

```
Array.prototype.reverse.call( a );
// still returns a String object wrapper (see Chapter 3)
// for "foo" :(
```

Another workaround (aka hack) is to convert the `string` into an array, perform the desired operation, then convert it back to a `string`:

```
var c = a
    // split `a` into an array of characters
    .split( "" )
    // reverse the array of characters
    .reverse()
    // join the array of characters back to a string
    .join( "" );

c; // "oof"
```

If that feels ugly, it is. Nevertheless, *it works* for simple `strings`, so if you need something quick-n-dirty, often such an approach gets the job done.

 Be careful! This approach doesn't work for `strings` with complex (unicode) characters in them (astral symbols, multibyte characters, etc.). You need more sophisticated library utilities that are unicode-aware for such operations to be handled accurately. Consult Mathias Bynens' work on the subject: Esrever (*https://github.com/ mathiasbynens/esrever*).

The other way to look at this is if you are more commonly doing tasks on your "strings" that treat them as basically *arrays of characters*, perhaps it's better to just actually store them as `arrays` rather than as `strings`. You'll probably save yourself a lot of hassle of converting from `string` to `array` each time. You can always call `join("")` on the `array` *of characters* whenever you actually need the `string` representation.

Numbers

JavaScript has just one numeric type: number. This type includes both "integer" values and fractional decimal numbers. I say "integer" in quotes because it's long been a criticism of JS that there's not true integers, as there are in other languages. That may change at some point in the future, but for now, we just have numbers for everything.

So, in JS, an "integer" is just a value that has no fractional decimal value. That is, 42.0 is as much an "integer" as 42.

Like most modern languages, including practically all scripting languages, the implementation of JavaScript's numbers is based on the "IEEE 754" standard, often called "floating-point." JavaScript specifically uses the "double precision" format (aka "64-bit binary") of the standard.

There are many great write-ups on the Web about the nitty-gritty details of how binary floating-point numbers are stored in memory, and the implications of those choices. Because understanding bit patterns in memory is not strictly necessary to understand how to correctly use numbers in JS, we'll leave it as an exercise for the interested reader if you'd like to dig further into IEEE 754 details.

Numeric Syntax

Number literals are expressed in JavaScript generally as base-10 decimal literals. For example:

```
var a = 42;
var b = 42.3;
```

The leading portion of a decimal value, if 0, is optional:

```
var a = 0.42;
var b = .42;
```

Similarly, the trailing portion (the fractional) of a decimal value after the ., if 0, is optional:

```
var a = 42.0;
var b = 42.;
```

42. is pretty uncommon, and probably not a great idea if you're trying to avoid confusion when other people read your code. But it is, nevertheless, valid.

By default, most numbers will be outputted as base-10 decimals, with trailing fractional 0s removed. So:

```
var a = 42.300;
var b = 42.0;

a; // 42.3
b; // 42
```

Very large or very small numbers will by default be outputted in exponent form, the same as the output of the toExponential() method, like:

```
var a = 5E10;
a;                   // 50000000000
a.toExponential();   // "5e+10"

var b = a * a;
b;                   // 2.5e+21

var c = 1 / a;
c;                   // 2e-11
```

Because number values can be boxed with the Number object wrapper (see Chapter 3), number values can access methods that are built into the Number.prototype (see Chapter 3). For example, the toFixed(..) method allows you to specify how many fractional decimal places you'd like the value to be represented with:

```
var a = 42.59;

a.toFixed( 0 ); // "43"
a.toFixed( 1 ); // "42.6"
a.toFixed( 2 ); // "42.59"
a.toFixed( 3 ); // "42.590"
a.toFixed( 4 ); // "42.5900"
```

Notice that the output is actually a string representation of the number, and that the value is 0-padded on the righthand side if you ask for more decimals than the value holds.

toPrecision(..) is similar, but specifies how many *significant digits* should be used to represent the value:

```
var a = 42.59;

a.toPrecision( 1 ); // "4e+1"
a.toPrecision( 2 ); // "43"
a.toPrecision( 3 ); // "42.6"
a.toPrecision( 4 ); // "42.59"
a.toPrecision( 5 ); // "42.590"
a.toPrecision( 6 ); // "42.5900"
```

You don't have to use a variable with the value in it to access these methods; you can access these methods directly on number literals. But you have to be careful with the . operator. Since . is a valid numeric character, it will first be interpreted as part of the number literal, if possible, instead of being interpreted as a property accessor:

```
// invalid syntax:
42.toFixed( 3 );    // SyntaxError

// these are all valid:
(42).toFixed( 3 );  // "42.000"
0.42.toFixed( 3 );  // "0.420"
42..toFixed( 3 );   // "42.000"
```

42.toFixed(3) is invalid syntax, because the . is swallowed up as part of the 42. literal (which is valid—see above!), and so then there's no . property operator present to make the .toFixed access.

42..toFixed(3) works because the first . is part of the number and the second . is the property operator. But it probably looks strange, and indeed it's very rare to see something like that in actual JavaScript code. In fact, it's pretty uncommon to access methods directly on any of the primitive values. Uncommon doesn't mean *bad* or *wrong*.

There are libraries that extend the built-in Num ber.prototype (see Chapter 3) to provide extra operations on/with numbers, and so in those cases, it's perfectly valid to use something like 10..makeItRain() to set off a 10-second money raining animation, or something else silly like that.

This is also technically valid (notice the space):

```
42 .toFixed(3); // "42.000"
```

However, with the number literal specifically, this is a particularly confusing coding style and will serve no other purpose but to confuse other developers (and your future self). Avoid it.

numbers can also be specified in exponent form, which is common when representing larger numbers, such as:

```
var onethousand = 1E3;                          // means 1 * 10^3
var onemilliononehundredthousand = 1.1E6;       // means 1.1 * 10^6
```

number literals can also be expressed in other bases, like binary, octal, and hexadecimal.

These formats work in current versions of JavaScript:

```
0xf3; // hexadecimal for: 243
0Xf3; // ditto

0363; // octal for: 243
```

 Starting with ES6 + strict mode, the 0363 form of octal literals is no longer allowed (see below for the new form). The 0363 form is still allowed in non-strict mode, but you should stop using it anyway, to be future-friendly (and because you should be using strict mode by now!).

As of ES6, the following new forms are also valid:

```
0o363;      // octal for: 243
0O363;      // ditto

0b11110011; // binary for: 243
0B11110011; // ditto
```

Please do your fellow developers a favor: never use the 0O363 form. 0 next to capital O is just asking for confusion. Always use the lowercase predicates 0x, 0b, and 0o.

Small Decimal Values

The most (in)famous side effect of using binary floating-point numbers (which, remember, is true of *all* languages that use IEEE 754—not *just* JavaScript as many assume/pretend) is:

```
0.1 + 0.2 === 0.3; // false
```

Mathematically, we know that statement should be `true`. Why is it `false`?

Simply put, the representations for `0.1` and `0.2` in binary floating point are not exact, so when they are added, the result is not exactly `0.3`. It's *really* close, `0.30000000000000004`, but if your comparison fails, "close" is irrelevant.

 Should JavaScript switch to a different number implementation that has exact representations for all values? Some think so. There have been many alternatives presented over the years. None of them have been accepted, and perhaps none will ever be. As easy as it may seem to just wave a hand and say, "Fix that bug already!", it's not nearly that easy. If it were, it most definitely would have been changed a long time ago.

Now, the question is, if some `numbers` can't be *trusted* to be exact, does that mean we can't use `numbers` at all? Of course not.

There are some applications where you need to be more careful, especially when dealing with fractional decimal values. There are also plenty of (maybe most?) applications that only deal with whole numbers ("integers"), and moreover, only deal with numbers in the millions or trillions at maximum. These applications have been, and always will be, perfectly safe to use numeric operations in JS.

What if we *did* need to compare two `numbers`, like `0.1 + 0.2` to `0.3`, knowing that the simple equality test fails?

The most commonly accepted practice is to use a tiny "rounding error" value as the *tolerance* for comparison. This tiny value is often called "machine epsilon," which is commonly 2^{-52} (`2.220446049250313e-16`) for the kind of `numbers` in JavaScript.

As of ES6, `Number.EPSILON` is predefined with this tolerance value, so you'd want to use it, but you can safely polyfill the definition for pre-ES6:

```
if (!Number.EPSILON) {
    Number.EPSILON = Math.pow(2,-52);
}
```

We can use this Number.EPSILON to compare two numbers for "equality" (within the rounding error tolerance):

```
function numbersCloseEnoughToEqual(n1,n2) {
    return Math.abs( n1 - n2 ) < Number.EPSILON;
}

var a = 0.1 + 0.2;
var b = 0.3;

numbersCloseEnoughToEqual( a, b );                      // true
numbersCloseEnoughToEqual( 0.0000001, 0.0000002 );     // false
```

The maximum floating-point value that can be represented is roughly 1.798e+308 (which is really, really, really huge!), predefined for you as Number.MAX_VALUE. On the small end, Number.MIN_VALUE is roughly 5e-324, which isn't negative but is really close to zero!

Safe Integer Ranges

Because of how numbers are represented, there is a range of "safe" values for the whole number "integers," and it's significantly less than Number.MAX_VALUE.

The maximum integer that can "safely" be represented (that is, there's a guarantee that the requested value is actually representable unambiguously) is 2^53 - 1, which is 9007199254740991. If you insert your commas, you'll see that this is just over 9 quadrillion. So that's pretty darn big for numbers to range up to.

This value is actually automatically predefined in ES6, as Num ber.MAX_SAFE_INTEGER. Unsurprisingly, there's a minimum value, -9007199254740991, and it's defined in ES6 as Num ber.MIN_SAFE_INTEGER.

The main scenario in which JS programs are confronted with such large numbers is when dealing with 64-bit IDs from databases, etc. 64-bit numbers cannot be represented accurately with the number type, so they must be stored in (and transmitted to/from) JavaScript using string representation.

Numeric operations on such large ID number values (besides comparison, which will be fine with strings) aren't all that common, thankfully. But if you *do* need to perform math on these very large values, for now you'll need to use a *big number* utility. Big numbers may get official support in a future version of JavaScript.

Testing for Integers

To test if a value is an integer, you can use the ES6-specified `Number.isInteger(..)`:

```
Number.isInteger( 42 );      // true
Number.isInteger( 42.000 ); // true
Number.isInteger( 42.3 );    // false
```

To polyfill `Number.isInteger(..)` for pre-ES6:

```
if (!Number.isInteger) {
    Number.isInteger = function(num) {
        return typeof num == "number" && num % 1 == 0;
    };
}
```

To test if a value is a *safe integer*, use the ES6-specified `Number.isSafeInteger(..)`:

```
Number.isSafeInteger( Number.MAX_SAFE_INTEGER );   // true
Number.isSafeInteger( Math.pow( 2, 53 ) );         // false
Number.isSafeInteger( Math.pow( 2, 53 ) - 1 );     // true
```

To polyfill `Number.isSafeInteger(..)` in pre-ES6 browsers:

```
if (!Number.isSafeInteger) {
    Number.isSafeInteger = function(num) {
        return Number.isInteger( num ) &&
            Math.abs( num ) <= Number.MAX_SAFE_INTEGER;
    };
}
```

32-Bit (Signed) Integers

While integers can range up to roughly 9 quadrillion safely (53 bits), there are some numeric operations (like the bitwise operators) that are only defined for 32-bit numbers, so the "safe range" for numbers used in that way must be much smaller.

The range then is `Math.pow(-2,31)` (-2147483648, about −2.1 billion) up to `Math.pow(2,31)-1` (2147483647, about +2.1 billion).

To force a number value in a to a 32-bit signed integer value, use a | 0. This works because the | bitwise operator only works for 32-bit integer values (meaning it can only pay attention to 32 bits and any other bits will be lost). Then, "or'ing" with zero is essentially a no-op bitwise speaking.

Certain special values (which we will cover in the next section) such as NaN and Infinity are not "32-bit safe," in that those values when passed to a bitwise operator will pass through the abstract operation ToInt32 (see Chapter 4) and become simply the +0 value for the purpose of that bitwise operation.

Special Values

There are several special values spread across the various types that the *alert* JS developer needs to be aware of, and use properly.

The Nonvalue Values

For the undefined type, there is one and only one value: undefined. For the null type, there is one and only one value: null. So for both of them, the label is both its type and its value.

Both undefined and null are often taken to be interchangeable as either "empty" values or "non" values. Other developers prefer to distinguish between them with nuance. For example:

- null is an empty value.
- undefined is a missing value.

Or:

- undefined hasn't had a value yet.
- null had a value and doesn't anymore.

Regardless of how you choose to "define" and use these two values, null is a special keyword, not an identifier, and thus you cannot treat it as a variable to assign to (why would you!?). However, unde fined *is* (unfortunately) an identifier. Uh oh.

Undefined

In non-strict mode, it's actually possible (though incredibly ill-advised!) to assign a value to the globally provided undefined identifier:

```
function foo() {
    undefined = 2; // really bad idea!
}

foo();

function foo() {
    "use strict";
    undefined = 2; // TypeError!
}

foo();
```

In both non-strict mode and strict mode, however, you can create a local variable of the name undefined. But again, this is a terrible idea!

```
function foo() {
    "use strict";
    var undefined = 2;
    console.log( undefined ); // 2
}

foo();
```

Friends don't let friends override undefined. Ever.

void operator

While undefined is a built-in identifier that holds (unless modified —see above!) the built-in undefined value, another way to get this value is the void operator.

The expression void ___ "voids" out any value, so that the result of the expression is always the undefined value. It doesn't modify the existing value; it just ensures that no value comes back from the operator expression:

```
var a = 42;

console.log( void a, a ); // undefined 42
```

By convention (mostly from C-language programming), to represent the undefined value standalone by using void, you'd use void 0 (though clearly even void true or any other void expression does the same thing). There's no practical difference between void 0, void 1, and undefined.

But the void operator can be useful in a few other circumstances, if you need to ensure that an expression has no result value (even if it has side effects).

For example:

```
function doSomething() {
    // note: `APP.ready` is provided by our application
    if (!APP.ready) {
        // try again later
        return void setTimeout( doSomething,100 );
    }

    var result;

    // do some other stuff
    return result;
}

// were we able to do it right away?
if (doSomething()) {
    // handle next tasks right away
}
```

Here, the setTimeout(..) function returns a numeric value (the unique identifier of the timer interval, if you wanted to cancel it), but we want to void that out so that the return value of our function doesn't give a false positive with the if statement.

Many devs prefer to just do these actions separately, which works the same but doesn't use the void operator:

```
if (!APP.ready) {
    // try again later
    setTimeout( doSomething,100 );
    return;
}
```

In general, if there's ever a place where a value exists (from some expression) and you'd find it useful for the value to be undefined instead, use the void operator. That probably won't be terribly common in your programs, but in the rare cases you do need it, it can be quite helpful.

Special Numbers

The number type includes several special values. We'll take a look at each in detail.

The not number, number

Any mathematic operation you perform without both operands being numbers (or values that can be interpreted as regular numbers in base 10 or base 16) will result in the operation failing to produce a valid number, in which case you will get the NaN value.

NaN literally stands for "not a number," though this label/description is very poor and misleading, as we'll see shortly. It would be much more accurate to think of NaN as being an "invalid number," "failed number," or even "bad number," than to think of it as "not a number."

For example:

```
var a = 2 / "foo";       // NaN

typeof a === "number";   // true
```

In other words, "the type of not-a-number is *number*!" Hooray for confusing names and semantics.

NaN is a kind of "sentinel value" (an otherwise normal value that's assigned a special meaning) that represents a special kind of error condition within the number set. The error condition is, in essence, "I tried to perform a mathematic operation but failed, so here's the failed number result instead."

So, if you have a value in some variable and want to test to see if it's this special failed-number NaN, you might think you could directly compare to NaN itself, as you can with any other value, like null or undefined. Nope.

```
var a = 2 / "foo";

a == NaN;    // false
a === NaN;   // false
```

NaN is a very special value in that it's never equal to another NaN value (i.e., it's never equal to itself). It's the only value, in fact, that is not reflexive (without the Identity characteristic x === x). So, NaN !== NaN. A bit strange, huh?

So how *do* we test for it, if we can't compare to NaN (since that comparison would always fail)?

```
var a = 2 / "foo";

isNaN( a ); // true
```

Easy enough, right? We use the built-in global utility called isNaN(..) and it tells us if the value is NaN or not. Problem solved!

Not so fast.

The isNaN(..) utility has a fatal flaw. It appears it tried to take the meaning of NaN ("Not a Number") too literally—that its job is basically, "test if the thing passed in is either not a number or is a number." But that's not quite accurate:

```
var a = 2 / "foo";
var b = "foo";

a; // NaN
b; "foo"

window.isNaN( a ); // true
window.isNaN( b ); // true--ouch!
```

Clearly, "foo" is literally *not a number*, but it's definitely not the NaN value either! This bug has been in JS since the very beginning (over 19 years of *ouch*).

As of ES6, finally a replacement utility has been provided: Number.isNaN(..). A simple polyfill for it so that you can safely check NaN values *now* even in pre-ES6 browsers is:

```
if (!Number.isNaN) {
    Number.isNaN = function(n) {
        return (
            typeof n === "number" &&
            window.isNaN( n )
        );
    };
}

var a = 2 / "foo";
var b = "foo";

Number.isNaN( a ); // true
Number.isNaN( b ); // false--phew!
```

Actually, we can implement a Number.isNaN(..) polyfill even easier, by taking advantage of that peculiar fact that NaN isn't equal to itself. NaN is the *only* value in the whole language where that's true; every other value is always *equal to itself*.

So:

```
if (!Number.isNaN) {
    Number.isNaN = function(n) {
        return n !== n;
    };
}
```

Weird, huh? But it works!

NaNs are probably a reality in a lot of real-world JS programs, either on purpose or by accident. It's a really good idea to use a reliable test, like Number.isNaN(..) as provided (or polyfilled), to recognize them properly.

If you're currently using just isNaN(..) in a program, the sad reality is your program *has a bug*, even if you haven't been bitten by it yet!

Infinities

Developers from traditional compiled languages like C are probably used to seeing either a compiler error or runtime exception, like "divide by zero," for an operation like:

```
var a = 1 / 0;
```

However, in JS, this operation is well-defined and results in the value Infinity (aka Number.POSITIVE_INFINITY). Unsurprisingly:

```
var a = 1 / 0;  // Infinity
var b = -1 / 0; // -Infinity
```

As you can see, -Infinity (aka Number.NEGATIVE_INFINITY) results from a divide-by-zero where either (but not both!) of the divide operands is negative.

JS uses finite numeric representations (IEEE 754 floating-point, which we covered earlier), so contrary to pure mathematics, it seems it *is* possible to overflow even with an operation like addition or subtraction, in which case you'd get Infinity or -Infinity.

For example:

```
var a = Number.MAX_VALUE;  // 1.7976931348623157e+308
a + a;                     // Infinity
a + Math.pow( 2, 970 );    // Infinity
a + Math.pow( 2, 969 );    // 1.7976931348623157e+308
```

According to the specification, if an operation like addition results in a value that's too big to represent, the IEEE 754 "round-tonearest" mode specifies what the result should be. So, in a crude sense, `Number.MAX_VALUE + Math.pow( 2, 969 )` is closer to `Number.MAX_VALUE` than to `Infinity`, so it "rounds down," whereas `Number.MAX_VALUE + Math.pow( 2, 970 )` is closer to `Infinity` so it "rounds up."

If you think too much about that, it's going to make your head hurt. So don't. Seriously, stop!

Once you overflow to either one of the *infinities*, however, there's no going back. In other words, in an almost poetic sense, you can go from finite to infinite but not from infinite back to finite.

It's almost philosophical to ask: "What is infinity divided by infinity?" Our naive brains would likely say "1" or maybe "infinity." Turns out neither is true. Both mathematically and in JavaScript, `Infinity / Infinity` is not a defined operation. In JS, this results in `NaN`.

But what about any positive finite `number` divided by `Infinity`? That's easy! `0`. And what about a negative finite `number` divided by `Infinity`? Keep reading!

Zeros

While it may confuse the mathematics-minded reader, JavaScript has both a normal zero `0` (otherwise known as a positive zero `+0`) *and* a negative zero `-0`. Before we explain why the `-0` exists, we should examine how JS handles it, because it can be quite confusing.

Besides being specified literally as `-0`, negative zero also results from certain mathematic operations. For example:

```
var a = 0 / -3; // -0
var b = 0 * -3; // -0
```

Addition and subtraction cannot result in a negative zero.

A negative zero when examined in the developer console will usually reveal `-0`, though that was not the common case until fairly recently, so some older browsers you encounter may still report it as `0`.

However, if you try to stringify a negative zero value, it will always be reported as `"0"`, according to the spec:

```
var a = 0 / -3;
```

```
// (some browser) consoles at least get it right
a;                          // -0

// but the spec insists on lying to you!
a.toString();               // "0"
a + "";                     // "0"
String( a );                // "0"

// strangely, even JSON gets in on the deception
JSON.stringify( a );   // "0"
```

Interestingly, the reverse operations (going from `string` to `number`) don't lie:

```
+"-0";                  // -0
Number( "-0" );         // -0
JSON.parse( "-0" ); // -0
```

 The `JSON.stringify( -0 )` behavior of `"0"` is particularly strange when you observe that it's inconsistent   with   the   reverse: `JSON.parse( "-0" )` reports `-0` as you'd correctly expect.

In addition to stringification of negative zero being deceptive to hide its true value, the comparison operators are also (intentionally) configured to *lie*:

```
var a = 0;
var b = 0 / -3;

a == b;     // true
-0 == 0;    // true

a === b;    // true
-0 === 0;   // true

0 > -0;     // false
a > b;      // false
```

Clearly, if you want to distinguish a `-0` from a `0` in your code, you can't just rely on what the developer console outputs, so you're going to have to be a bit more clever:

```
function isNegZero(n) {
    n = Number( n );
    return (n === 0) && (1 / n === -Infinity);
}
```

```
isNegZero( -0 );        // true
isNegZero( 0 / -3 );    // true
isNegZero( 0 );         // false
```

Now, why do we need a negative zero, besides academic trivia?

There are certain applications where developers use the magnitude of a value to represent one piece of information (like speed of movement per animation frame) and the sign of that number to represent another piece of information (like the direction of that movement).

In those applications, as one example, if a variable arrives at zero and it loses its sign, then you would lose the information of what direction it was moving in before it arrived at zero. Preserving the sign of the zero prevents potentially unwanted information loss.

Special Equality

As we saw above, the NaN value and the -0 value have special behavior when it comes to equality comparison. NaN is never equal to itself, so you have to use ES6's Number.isNaN(..) (or a polyfill). Simlarly, -0 lies and pretends that it's equal (even === strict equal— see Chapter 4) to regular 0, so you have to use the somewhat hackish isNegZero(..) utility we suggested above.

As of ES6, there's a new utility that can be used to test two values for absolute equality, without any of these exceptions. It's called Object.is(..):

```
var a = 2 / "foo";
var b = -3 * 0;

Object.is( a, NaN );    // true
Object.is( b, -0 );     // true

Object.is( b, 0 );      // false
```

There's a pretty simple polyfill for Object.is(..) for pre-ES6 environments:

```
if (!Object.is) {
    Object.is = function(v1, v2) {
        // test for `-0`
        if (v1 === 0 && v2 === 0) {
            return 1 / v1 === 1 / v2;
        }
        // test for `NaN`
        if (v1 !== v1) {
```

```
        return v2 !== v2;
    }
    // everything else
    return v1 === v2;
};
}
```

`Object.is(..)` probably shouldn't be used in cases where `==` or `===` are known to be *safe* (see Chapter 4), as the operators are likely much more efficient and certainly are more idiomatic/common. `Object.is(..)` is mostly for these special cases of equality.

Value Versus Reference

In many other languages, values can either be assigned/passed by value-copy or by reference-copy depending on the syntax you use.

For example, in C++ if you want to pass a `number` variable into a function and have that variable's value updated, you can declare the function parameter like `int& myNum`, and when you pass in a variable like `x`, `myNum` will be a reference to `x`; references are like a special form of pointers, where you obtain a pointer to another variable (like an *alias*). If you don't declare a reference parameter, the value passed in will *always* be copied, even if it's a complex object.

In JavaScript, there are no pointers, and references work a bit differently. You cannot have a reference from one JS variable to another variable. That's just not possible.

A reference in JS points at a (shared) value, so if you have 10 different references, they are all always distinct references to a single shared value; *none of them are references/pointers to each other*.

Moreover, in JavaScript, there are no syntactic hints that control value versus reference assignment/passing. Instead, the *type* of the value *solely* controls whether that value will be assigned by value-copy or by reference-copy.

Let's illustrate:

```
var a = 2;
var b = a; // `b` is always a copy of the value in `a`
b++;
a; // 2
b; // 3

var c = [1,2,3];
```

```
var d = c; // `d` is a reference to the shared `[1,2,3]` value
d.push( 4 );
c; // [1,2,3,4]
d; // [1,2,3,4]
```

Simple values (aka scalar primitives) are *always* assigned/passed by
value-copy: null, undefined, string, number, boolean, and ES6's
symbol.

Compound values—objects (including arrays, and all boxed object
wrappers—see Chapter 3) and functions—*always* create a copy of
the reference on assignment or passing.

In the above snippet, because 2 is a scalar primitive, a holds one initial copy of that value, and b is assigned another *copy* of the value.
When changing b, you are in no way changing the value in a.

But both c and d are separate references to the same shared value
[1,2,3], which is a compound value. It's important to note that neither c nor d more "owns" the [1,2,3] value—both are just equal
peer references to the value. So, when using either reference to modify (.push(4)) the actual shared array value itself, it's affecting just
the one shared value, and both references will reference the newly
modified value [1,2,3,4].

Since references point to the values themselves and not to the variables, you cannot use one reference to change where another reference is pointed:

```
var a = [1,2,3];
var b = a;
a; // [1,2,3]
b; // [1,2,3]

// later
b = [4,5,6];
a; // [1,2,3]
b; // [4,5,6]
```

When we make the assignment b = [4,5,6], we are doing absolutely nothing to affect *where* a is still referencing ([1,2,3]). To do
that, b would have to be a pointer to a rather than a reference to the
array—but no such capability exists in JS!

The most common way such confusion happens is with function
parameters:

```
function foo(x) {
    x.push( 4 );
    x; // [1,2,3,4]

    // later
    x = [4,5,6];
    x.push( 7 );
    x; // [4,5,6,7]
}

var a = [1,2,3];

foo( a );

a; // [1,2,3,4]  not  [4,5,6,7]
```

When we pass in the argument a, it assigns a copy of the a reference to x. x and a are separate references pointing at the same [1,2,3] value. Now, inside the function, we can use that reference to mutate the value itself (push(4)). But when we make the assignment x = [4,5,6], this is in no way affecting where the initial reference a is pointing—it still points at the (now modified) [1,2,3,4] value.

There is no way to use the x reference to change where a is pointing. We could only modify the contents of the shared value that both a and x are pointing to.

To accomplish changing a to have the [4,5,6,7] value contents, you can't create a new array and assign—you must modify the existing array value:

```
function foo(x) {
    x.push( 4 );
    x; // [1,2,3,4]

    // later
    x.length = 0; // empty existing array in-place
    x.push( 4, 5, 6, 7 );
    x; // [4,5,6,7]
}

var a = [1,2,3];

foo( a );

a; // [4,5,6,7] not [1,2,3,4]
```

As you can see, x.length = 0 and x.push(4,5,6,7) were not creating a new array, but modifying the existing shared array. So of course, a references the new [4,5,6,7] contents.

Remember: you cannot directly control/override value-copy versus reference—those semantics are controlled entirely by the type of the underlying value.

To effectively pass a compound value (like an array) by value-copy, you need to manually make a copy of it, so that the reference passed doesn't still point to the original. For example:

```
foo( a.slice() );
```

slice(..) with no parameters by default makes an entirely new (shallow) copy of the array. So, we pass in a reference only to the copied array, and thus foo(..) cannot affect the contents of a.

To do the reverse—pass a scalar primitive value in a way where its value updates can be seen, kinda like a reference—you have to wrap the value in another compound value (object, array, etc.) that *can* be passed by reference-copy:

```
function foo(wrapper) {
    wrapper.a = 42;
}

var obj = {
    a: 2
};

foo( obj );

obj.a; // 42
```

Here, obj acts as a wrapper for the scalar primitive property a. When passed to foo(..), a copy of the obj reference is passed in and set to the wrapper parameter. We now can use the wrapper reference to access the shared object, and update its property. After the function finishes, obj.a will see the updated value 42.

It may occur to you that if you wanted to pass in a reference to a scalar primitive value like 2, you could just box the value in its Number object wrapper (see Chapter 3).

It *is* true a copy of the reference to this Number object *will* be passed to the function, but unfortunately, having a reference to the shared object is not going to give you the ability to modify the shared primitive value, like you may expect:

```
function foo(x) {
    x = x + 1;
    x; // 3
}

var a = 2;
var b = new Number( a ); // or equivalently `Object(a)`

foo( b );
console.log( b ); // 2, not 3
```

The problem is that the underlying scalar primitive value is *not mutable* (same goes for String and Boolean). If a Number object holds the scalar primitive value 2, that exact Number object can never be changed to hold another value; you can only create a whole new Number object with a different value.

When x is used in the expression x + 1, the underlying scalar primitive value 2 is unboxed (extracted) from the Number object automatically, so the line x = x + 1 very subtly changes x from being a shared reference to the Number object, to just holding the scalar primitive value 3 as a result of the addition operation 2 + 1. Therefore, b on the outside still references the original unmodified/immutable Number object holding the value 2.

You *can* add properties on top of the Number object (just not change its inner primitive value), so you could exchange information indirectly via those additional properties.

This is not all that common, however; it probably would not be considered a good practice by most developers.

Instead of using the wrapper object Number in this way, it's probably much better to use the manual object wrapper (obj) approach in the earlier snippet. That's not to say that there are no clever uses for the boxed object wrappers like Number—just that you should probably prefer the scalar primitive value form in most cases.

References are quite powerful, but sometimes they get in your way, and sometimes you need them where they don't exist. The only control you have over reference versus value-copy behavior is the type of the value itself, so you must indirectly influence the assignment/passing behavior by which value types you choose to use.

Review

In JavaScript, arrays are simply numerically indexed collections of any value type. strings are somewhat "array-like," but they have distinct behaviors and care must be taken if you want to treat them as arrays. Numbers in JavaScript include both "integers" and floating-point values.

Several special values are defined within the primitive types.

The null type has just one value, null, and likewise the undefined type has just the undefined value. undefined is basically the default value in any variable or property if no other value is present. The void operator lets you create the undefined value from any other value.

numbers include several special values, like NaN (supposedly "Not a Number," but really more appropriately "invalid number"); +Infinity and -Infinity; and -0.

Simple scalar primitives (strings, numbers, etc.) are assigned/passed by value-copy, but compound values (objects, etc.) are assigned/passed by reference-copy. References are not like references/pointers in other languages—they're never pointed at other variables/references, only at the underlying values.

CHAPTER 3

Natives

Several times in Chapters 1 and 2, we alluded to various built-ins, usually called "natives," like String and Number. Let's examine those in detail now.

Here's a list of the most commonly used natives:

- String()
- Number()
- Boolean()
- Array()
- Object()
- Function()
- RegExp()
- Date()
- Error()
- Symbol()—added in ES6!

As you can see, these natives are actually built-in functions.

If you're coming to JS from a language like Java, JavaScript's String() will look like the String(..) constructor you're used to for creating string values. So, you'll quickly observe that you can do things like:

```
var s = new String( "Hello World!" );

console.log( s.toString() ); // "Hello World!"
```

It *is* true that each of these natives can be used as a native constructor. But what's being constructed may be different than you think:

```
var a = new String( "abc" );

typeof a;                          // "object" ... not "String"

a instanceof String;               // true

Object.prototype.toString.call( a ); // "[object String]"
```

The result of the constructor form of value creation (new String("abc")) is an object wrapper around the primitive ("abc") value.

Importantly, typeof shows that these objects are not their own special *types*, but more appropriately they are subtypes of the object type.

This object wrapper can further be observed with:

```
console.log( a );
```

The output of that statement varies depending on your browser, as developer consoles are free to choose however they feel it's appropriate to serialize the object for developer inspection.

 At the time of writing, the latest Chrome prints something like this: String {0: "a", 1: "b", 2: "c", length: 3, [[PrimitiveValue]]: "abc"}. But older versions of Chrome used to just print this: String {0: "a", 1: "b", 2: "c"}. The latest Firefox currently prints String ["a","b","c"], but used to print "abc" in italics, which was clickable to open the object inspector. Of course, these results are subject to rapid change and your experience may vary.

The point is, new String("abc") creates a string wrapper object around "abc", not just the primitive "abc" value itself.

Internal [[Class]]

Values that are typeof of "object" (such as an array) are additionally tagged with an internal [[Class]] property (think of this more as an internal *class*ification rather than related to classes from traditional class-oriented coding). This property cannot be accessed directly, but can generally can be revealed indirectly by borrowing the default Object.prototype.toString(..) method called against the value. For example:

```
Object.prototype.toString.call( [1,2,3] );
// "[object Array]"

Object.prototype.toString.call( /regex-literal/i );
// "[object RegExp]"
```

So, for the array in this example, the internal [[Class]] value is "Array", and for the regular expression, it's "RegExp". In most cases, this internal [Class]] value corresponds to the built-in native constructor (see below) that's related to the value, but that's not always the case.

What about primitive values? First, null and undefined:

```
Object.prototype.toString.call( null );
// "[object Null]"

Object.prototype.toString.call( undefined );
// "[object Undefined]"
```

You'll note that there are no Null() or Undefined() native constructors, but nevertheless "Null" and "Undefined" are the internal [[Class]] values exposed.

But for the other simple primitives like string, number, and boolean, another behavior actually kicks in, which is usually called "boxing" (see "Boxing Wrappers" on page 42):

```
Object.prototype.toString.call( "abc" );
// "[object String]"

Object.prototype.toString.call( 42 );
// "[object Number]"

Object.prototype.toString.call( true );
// "[object Boolean]"
```

In this snippet, each of the simple primitives are automatically boxed by their respective object wrappers, which is why `"String"`, `"Number"`, and `"Boolean"` are revealed as the respective internal `[[Class]]` values.

 The behavior of `toString()` and `[[Class]]` as illustrated here has changed a bit from ES5 to ES6, but we cover those details in the *ES6 & Beyond* title in this series.

Boxing Wrappers

These object wrappers serve a very important purpose. Primitive values don't have properties or methods, so to access `.length` or `.toString()` you need an object wrapper around the value. Thankfully, JS will automatically *box* (aka wrap) the primitive value to fulfill such accesses:

```
var a = "abc";

a.length; // 3
a.toUpperCase(); // "ABC"
```

So, if you're going to be accessing these properties/methods on your string values regularly, like an `i < a.length` condition in a `for` loop for instance, it might seem to make sense to just have the object form of the value from the start, so the JS engine doesn't need to implicitly create it for you.

But it turns out that's a bad idea. Browsers long ago performance-optimized the common cases like `.length`, which means your program will *actually go slower* if you try to "preoptimize" by directly using the object form (which isn't on the optimized path).

In general, there's basically no reason to use the object form directly. It's better to just let the boxing happen implicitly where necessary. In other words, never do things like `new String("abc")`, `new Number(42)`, etc.—always prefer using the literal primitive values `"abc"` and 42.

Object Wrapper Gotchas

There are even gotchas with using the object wrappers directly that you should be aware of if you *do* choose to ever use them.

For example, consider `Boolean` wrapped values:

```
var a = new Boolean( false );

if (!a) {
    console.log( "Oops" ); // never runs
}
```

The problem is that you've created an object wrapper around the `false` value, but objects themselves are "truthy" (see Chapter 4), so using the object behaves oppositely to using the underlying `false` value itself, which is quite contrary to normal expectation.

If you want to manually box a primitive value, you can use the `Object(..)` function (no `new` keyword):

```
var a = "abc";
var b = new String( a );
var c = Object( a );

typeof a; // "string"
typeof b; // "object"
typeof c; // "object"

b instanceof String; // true
c instanceof String; // true

Object.prototype.toString.call( b ); // "[object String]"
Object.prototype.toString.call( c ); // "[object String]"
```

Again, using the boxed object wrapper directly (like b and c above) is usually discouraged, but there may be some rare occasions you'll run into where they may be useful.

Unboxing

If you have an object wrapper and you want to get the underlying primitive value out, you can use the `valueOf()` method:

```
var a = new String( "abc" );
var b = new Number( 42 );
var c = new Boolean( true );

a.valueOf(); // "abc"
b.valueOf(); // 42
c.valueOf(); // true
```

Unboxing can also happen implicitly, when using an object wrapper value in a way that requires the primitive value. This process (coercion) will be covered in more detail in Chapter 4, but briefly:

```
var a = new String( "abc" );
var b = a + ""; // `b` has the unboxed primitive value "abc"

typeof a;        // "object"
typeof b;        // "string"
```

Natives as Constructors

For array, object, function, and regular-expression values, it's almost universally preferred that you use the literal form for creating the values, but the literal form creates the same sort of object as the constructor form does (that is, there is no nonwrapped value).

Just as we've seen above with the other natives, these constructor forms should generally be avoided, unless you really know you need them, mostly because they introduce exceptions and gotchas that you probably don't really *want* to deal with.

Array(..)

```
var a = new Array( 1, 2, 3 );
a; // [1, 2, 3]

var b = [1, 2, 3];
b; // [1, 2, 3]
```

 The Array(..) constructor does not require the new keyword in front of it. If you omit it, it will behave as if you have used it anyway. So Array(1,2,3) is the same outcome as new Array(1,2,3).

The Array constructor has a special form where if only one number argument is passed, instead of providing that value as *contents* of the array, it's taken as a length to "presize the array" (well, sorta).

This is a terrible idea. Firstly, you can trip over that form accidentally, as it's easy to forget.

But more importantly, there's no such thing as actually presizing the array. Instead, what you're creating is an otherwise empty array, but setting the length property of the array to the numeric value specified.

An array that has no explicit values in its slots, but has a length property that *implies* the slots exist, is a weird exotic type of data structure in JS with some very strange and confusing behavior. The capability to create such a value comes purely from old, deprecated, historical functionalities ("array-like objects" like the arguments object).

An array with at least one "empty slot" in it is often called a "sparse array."

It doesn't help matters that this is yet another example where browser developer consoles vary on how they represent such an object, which breeds more confusion.

For example:

```
var a = new Array( 3 );

a.length; // 3
a;
```

The serialization of a in Chrome is (at the time of writing) [undefined x 3]. This is really unfortunate. It implies that there are three undefined values in the slots of this array, when in fact the slots do not exist (so-called "empty slots"—also a bad name!).

To visualize the difference, try this:

```
var a = new Array( 3 );
var b = [ undefined, undefined, undefined ];
var c = [];
c.length = 3;

a;
b;
c;
```

As you can see with c in this example, empty slots in an array can happen after creation of the array. When changing the length of an array to go beyond its number of actually defined slot values, you implicitly introduce empty slots. In fact, you could even call delete b[1] in the above snippet, and it would introduce an empty slot into the middle of b.

For b (in Chrome, currently), you'll find [undefined, undefined, undefined] as the serialization, as opposed to [undefined x 3] for a and c. Confused? Yeah, so is everyone else.

Worse than that, at the time of writing, Firefox reports [, , ,] for a and c. Did you catch why that's so confusing? Look closely. Three commas implies four slots, not three slots like we'd expect.

What!? Firefox puts an extra , on the end of their serialization here because as of ES5, trailing commas in lists (array values, property lists, etc.) are allowed (and thus dropped and ignored). So if you were to type a [, , ,] value into your program or the console, you'd actually get the underlying value that's like [, ,] (that is, an array with three empty slots). This choice, while confusing if reading the developer console, is defended as instead making copy-n-paste behavior accurate.

If you're shaking your head or rolling your eyes about now, you're not alone! Shrugs.

Firefox appears to be changing their output in this scenario to Array [<3 empty slots>], which is certainly a big improvement over [, , ,].

Unfortunately, it gets worse. More than just confusing console output, a and b from the above code snippet actually behave the same in some cases but differently in others:

```
a.join( "-" ); // "--"
b.join( "-" ); // "--"

a.map(function(v,i){ return i; }); // [ undefined x 3 ]
b.map(function(v,i){ return i; }); // [ 0, 1, 2 ]
```

Ugh.

The a.map(..) call *fails* because the slots don't actually exist, so map(..) has nothing to iterate over. join(..) works differently. Basically, we can think of it implemented sort of like this:

```
function fakeJoin(arr,connector) {
    var str = "";
    for (var i = 0; i < arr.length; i++) {
        if (i > 0) {
            str += connector;
        }
        if (arr[i] !== undefined) {
            str += arr[i];
        }
    }
    return str;
}

var a = new Array( 3 );
fakeJoin( a, "-" ); // "--"
```

As you can see, join(..) works by just *assuming* the slots exist and looping up to the length value. Whatever map(..) does internally, it (apparently) doesn't make such an assumption, so the result from the strange "empty slots" array is unexpected and likely to cause failure.

So, if you wanted to *actually* create an array of actual undefined values (not just "empty slots"), how could you do it (besides manually)?

```
var a = Array.apply( null, { length: 3 } );
a; // [ undefined, undefined, undefined ]
```

Confused? Yeah. Here's roughly how it works.

apply(..) is a utility available to all functions, which calls the function it's used with but in a special way.

The first argument is a this object binding (covered in the *this & Object Prototypes* title in this series), which we don't care about here, so we set it to null. The second argument is supposed to be an array (or something *like* an array—aka an "array-like object"). The contents of this "array" are "spread" out as arguments to the function in question.

So, Array.apply(..) is calling the Array(..) function and spreading out the values (of the { length: 3 } object value) as its arguments.

Inside of apply(..), we can envision there's another for loop (kinda like join(..) from above) that goes from 0 up to, but not including, length (3 in our case).

For each index, it retrieves that key from the object. So if the array-object parameter was named arr internally inside of the apply(..) function, the property access would effectively be arr[0], arr[1], and arr[2]. Of course, none of those properties exist on the { length: 3 } object value, so all three of those property accesses would return the value undefined.

In other words, it ends up calling Array(..) basically like this: Array(undefined,undefined,undefined), which is how we end up with an array filled with undefined values, and not just those (crazy) empty slots.

While Array.apply(null, { length: 3 }) is a strange and verbose way to create an array filled with undefined values, it's *vastly* better and more reliable than what you get with the footgun'ish Array(3) empty slots.

Bottom line: *never ever, under any circumstances*, should you intentionally create and use these exotic empty-slot arrays. Just don't do it. They're nuts.

Object(..), Function(..), and RegExp(..)

The Object(..)/Function(..)/RegExp(..) constructors are also generally optional (and thus should usually be avoided unless specifically called for):

```
var c = new Object();
c.foo = "bar";
c; // { foo: "bar" }

var d = { foo: "bar" };
d; // { foo: "bar" }

var e = new Function( "a", "return a * 2;" );
var f = function(a) { return a * 2; }
function g(a) { return a * 2; }

var h = new RegExp( "^a*b+", "g" );
var i = /^a*b+/g;
```

There's practically no reason to ever use the `new Object()` constructor form, especially since it forces you to add properties one by one instead of many at once in the object literal form.

The `Function` constructor is helpful only in the rarest of cases, where you need to dynamically define a function's parameters and/or its function body. Do not just treat `Function(..)` as an alternate form of `eval(..)`. You will almost never need to dynamically define a function in this way.

Regular expressions defined in the literal form (`/^a*b+/g`) are strongly preferred, not just for ease of syntax but for performance reasons—the JS engine precompiles and caches them before code execution. Unlike the other constructor forms we've seen so far, `RegExp(..)` has some reasonable utility: to dynamically define the pattern for a regular expression:

```
var name = "Kyle";
var namePattern = new RegExp( "\\b(?:" + name + ")+\\b", "ig" );

var matches = someText.match( namePattern );
```

This kind of scenario legitimately occurs in JS programs from time to time, so you'd need to use the `new RegExp("pattern","flags")` form.

Date(..) and Error(..)

The `Date(..)` and `Error(..)` native constructors are much more useful than the other natives, because there is no literal form for either.

To create a date object value, you must use `new Date()`. The `Date(..)` constructor accepts optional arguments to specify the date/time to use, but if omitted, the current date/time is assumed.

By far the most common reason you construct a date object is to get the current Unix timestamp value (an integer number of seconds since Jan 1, 1970). You can do this by calling `getTime()` on a date object instance.

But an even easier way is to just call the static helper function defined as of ES5: `Date.now()`. And to polyfill that for pre-ES5 is pretty easy:

```
if (!Date.now) {
    Date.now = function(){
        return (new Date()).getTime();
    };
}
```

 If you call Date() without new, you'll get back a
string representation of the date/time at that
moment. The exact form of this representation
is not specified in the language spec, though
browsers tend to agree on something close to
`"Fri Jul 18 2014 00:31:02 GMT-0500
(CDT)"`.

The Error(..) constructor (much like Array() above) behaves the
same with the new keyword present or omitted.

The main reason you'd want to create an error object is that it cap-
tures the current execution stack context into the object (in most JS
engines, revealed as a read-only .stack property once constructed).
This stack context includes the function call stack and the line number where the error object was created, which makes debugging that
error much easier.

You would typically use such an error object with the throw operator:

```
function foo(x) {
    if (!x) {
        throw new Error( "x wasn't provided" );
    }
    // ..
}
```

Error object instances generally have at least a message property,
and sometimes other properties (which you should treat as read-
only), like type. However, other than inspecting the above-
mentioned stack property, it's usually best to just call toString()
on the error object (either explicitly, or implicitly through coercion
—see Chapter 4) to get a friendly formatted error message.

Technically, in addition to the general Error(..) native, there are several other specific-error-type natives: EvalError(..), RangeError(..), ReferenceError(..), SyntaxError(..), TypeError(..), and URIError(..). But it's very rare to manually use these specific error natives. They are automatically used if your program actually suffers from a real exception (such as referencing an undeclared variable and getting a ReferenceError error).

Symbol(..)

New as of ES6, an additional primitive value type has been added, called "Symbol." Symbols are special "unique" (not strictly guaranteed!) values that can be used as properties on objects with little fear of any collision. They're primarily designed for special built-in behaviors of ES6 constructs, but you can also define your own symbols.

Symbols can be used as property names, but you cannot see or access the actual value of a symbol from your program, nor from the developer console. If you evaluate a symbol in the developer console, what's shown looks like Symbol(Symbol.create), for example.

There are several predefined symbols in ES6, accessed as static properties of the Symbol function object, like Symbol.create, Symbol.iterator, etc. To use them, do something like:

```
obj[Symbol.iterator] = function(){ /*..*/ };
```

To define your own custom symbols, use the Symbol(..) native. The Symbol(..) native "constructor" is unique in that you're not allowed to use new with it, as doing so will throw an error:

```
var mysym = Symbol( "my own symbol" );
mysym;                // Symbol(my own symbol)
mysym.toString();     // "Symbol(my own symbol)"
typeof mysym;         // "symbol"

var a = { };
a[mysym] = "foobar";

Object.getOwnPropertySymbols( a );
// [ Symbol(my own symbol) ]
```

While symbols are not actually private (`Object.getOwnPropertySym bols(..)` reflects on the object and reveals the symbols quite publicly), using them for private or special properties is likely their primary use case. For most developers, they may take the place of property names with underscore (_) prefixes, which are almost always by convention signals to say, "Hey, this is a private/special/ internal property, so leave it alone!"

Symbols are *not* objects, they are simple scalar primitives.

Native Prototypes

Each of the built-in native constructors has its own `.prototype` object — `Array.prototype`, `String.prototype`, etc.

These objects contain behavior unique to their particular object subtype.

For example, all string objects, and by extension (via boxing) `string` primitives, have access to default behavior as methods defined on the `String.prototype` object.

By documentation convention, `String.proto type.XYZ` is shortened to `String#XYZ`, and likewise for all the other `.prototypes`.

String#indexOf(..)
Find the position in the string of another substring

String#charAt(..)
Access the character at a position in the string

String#substr(..), String#substring(..), *and* String#slice(..)
Extract a portion of the string as a new string

String#toUpperCase() *and* String#toLowerCase()
Create a new string that's converted to either uppercase or lowercase

```
String#trim()
```
   Create a new string that's stripped of any trailing or leading whitespace

None of the methods modify the string *in place*. Modifications (like case conversion or trimming) create a new value from the existing value.

By virtue of prototype delegation (see the *this & Object Prototypes* title in this series), any string value can access these methods:

```
var a = " abc ";

a.indexOf( "c" ); // 3
a.toUpperCase(); // " ABC "
a.trim();        // "abc"
```

The other constructor prototypes contain behaviors appropriate to their types, such as `Number#toFixed(..)` (stringifying a number with a fixed number of decimal digits) and `Array#concat(..)` (merging arrays). All functions have access to `apply(..)`, `call(..)`, and `bind(..)` because `Function.prototype` defines them.

But, some of the native prototypes aren't *just* plain objects:

```
typeof Function.prototype;            // "function"
Function.prototype();                 // it's an empty function!

RegExp.prototype.toString();          // "/(?:)/" -- empty regex
"abc".match( RegExp.prototype );      // [""]
```

A particularly bad idea, you can even modify these native prototypes (not just adding properties as you're probably familiar with):

```
Array.isArray( Array.prototype );   // true
Array.prototype.push( 1, 2, 3 );    // 3
Array.prototype;                    // [1,2,3]

// don't leave it that way, though, or expect weirdness!
// reset the `Array.prototype` to empty
Array.prototype.length = 0;
```

As you can see, `Function.prototype` is a function, `RegExp.proto type` is a regular expression, and `Array.prototype` is an array. Interesting and cool, huh?

Prototypes as defaults

`Function.prototype` being an empty function, `RegExp.prototype` being an "empty" (e.g., nonmatching) regex, and `Array.prototype` being an empty array make them all nice "default" values to assign to variables if those variables wouldn't already have had a value of the proper type.

For example:

```
function isThisCool(vals,fn,rx) {
    vals = vals || Array.prototype;
    fn = fn || Function.prototype;
    rx = rx || RegExp.prototype;

    return rx.test(
        vals.map( fn ).join( "" )
    );
}

isThisCool();        // true

isThisCool(
    ["a","b","c"],
    function(v){ return v.toUpperCase(); },
    /D/
);                   // false
```

As of ES6, we don't need to use the `vals = vals || ..` default value syntax trick (see Chapter 4) anymore, because default values can be set for parameters via native syntax in the function declaration (see Chapter 5).

One minor side benefit of this approach is that the `.prototypes` are already created and built-in; thus they are created *only once*. By contrast, using `[]`, `function(){}`, and `/(?:)/` values themselves for those defaults would (likely, depending on engine implementations) be re-creating those values (and probably garbage-collecting them later) for *each call* of `isThisCool(..)`. That could waste memory/CPU.

Also, be very careful not to use `Array.prototype` as a default value that will subsequently be modified. In this example, `vals` is used read-only, but if you were to instead make in-place changes to `vals`, you would actually be modifying `Array.prototype` itself, which would lead to the gotchas mentioned earlier!

 While we're pointing out these native prototypes and some usefulness, be cautious of relying on them and even more wary of modifying them in any way. See "Native Prototypes" on page 167 in Appendix A for more discussion.

Review

JavaScript provides object wrappers around primitive values, known as natives (`String`, `Number`, `Boolean`, etc). These object wrappers give the values access to behaviors appropriate for each object subtype (`String#trim()` and `Array#concat(..)`).

If you have a simple scalar primitive value like `"abc"` and you access its `length` property or some `String.prototype` method, JS automatically "boxes" the value (wraps it in its respective object wrapper) so that the property/method accesses can be fulfilled.

CHAPTER 4

Coercion

Now that we much more fully understand JavaScript's types and values, we turn our attention to a very controversial topic: coercion.

As we mentioned in Chapter 1, the debates over whether coercion is a useful feature or a flaw in the design of the language (or somewhere in between!) have raged since day one. If you've read other popular books on JS, you know that the overwhelmingly prevalent *message* out there is that coercion is magical, evil, confusing, and just downright a bad idea.

In the same overall spirit of this series, rather than running away from coercion because everyone else does, or because you get bitten by some quirk, I think you should run toward that which you don't understand and seek to *get it* more fully.

Our goal is to fully explore the pros and cons (yes, there *are* pros!) of coercion, so that you can make an informed decision on its appropriateness in your program.

Converting Values

Converting a value from one type to another is often called "type casting," when done explicitly, and "coercion" when done implicitly (forced by the rules of how a value is used).

It may not be obvious, but JavaScript coercions always result in one of the scalar primitive (see Chapter 2) values, like `string`, `number`, or `boolean`. There is no coercion that results in a complex value like `object` or `function`. Chapter 3 covers "boxing," which wraps scalar primitive values in their `object` counterparts, but this is not really coercion in an accurate sense.

Another way these terms are often distinguished is as follows: "type casting" (or "type conversion") occurs in statically typed languages at compile time, while "type coercion" is a runtime conversion for dynamically typed languages.

However, in JavaScript, most people refer to all these types of conversions as *coercion,* so the way I prefer to distinguish is to say "implicit coercion" versus "explicit coercion."

The difference should be obvious: "explicit coercion" is when it is obvious from looking at the code that a type conversion is intentionally occurring, whereas "implicit coercion" is when the type conversion will occur as a less obvious side effect of some other intentional operation.

For example, consider these two approaches to coercion:

```
var a = 42;

var b = a + "";      // implicit coercion

var c = String( a ); // explicit coercion
```

For b, the coercion that occurs happens implicitly, because the + operator combined with one of the operands being a `string` value (`""`) will insist on the operation being a `string` concatenation (adding two strings together), which *as a (hidden) side effect* will force the 42 value in a to be coerced to its `string` equivalent: `"42"`.

By contrast, the `String(..)` function makes it pretty obvious that it's explicitly taking the value in a and coercing it to a `string` representation.

Both approaches accomplish the same effect: `"42"` comes from 42. But it's the *how* that is at the heart of the heated debates over JavaScript coercion.

Technically, there's some nuanced behavioral difference here beyond the stylistic difference. We cover that in more detail later in the chapter, in "Implicitly: Strings <--> Numbers" on page 87.

The terms "explicit" and "implicit," or "obvious" and "hidden side effect," are *relative*.

If you know exactly what a + "" is doing and you're intentionally doing that to coerce to a string, you might feel the operation is sufficiently "explicit." Conversely, if you've never seen the String(..) function used for string coercion, its behavior might seem hidden enough as to feel "implicit" to you.

But we're having this discussion of "explicit" versus "implicit" based on the likely opinions of an *average, reasonably informed, but not expert or JS specification devotee* developer. To whatever extent you do or do not find yourself fitting neatly in that bucket, you will need to adjust your perspective on our observations here accordingly.

Just remember: it's often rare that we write our code and are the only ones who ever read it. Even if you're an expert on all the ins and outs of JS, consider how a less experienced teammate of yours will feel when they read your code. Will it be "explicit" or "implicit" to them in the same way it is for you?

Abstract Value Operations

Before we can explore *explicit* versus *implicit* coercion, we need to learn the basic rules that govern how values *become* either a string, number, or boolean. The ES5 spec in section 9 defines several "abstract operations" (fancy spec-speak for "internal-only operation") with the rules of value conversion. We will specifically pay attention to ToString, ToNumber, and ToBoolean, and to a lesser extent, ToPrimitive.

ToString

When any non-string value is coerced to a string representation, the conversion is handled by the ToString abstract operation in section 9.8 of the specification.

Built-in primitive values have natural stringification: null becomes "null", undefined becomes "undefined", and true becomes "true". numbers are generally expressed in the natural way you'd expect, but as we discussed in Chapter 2, very small or very large numbers are represented in exponent form:

```
// multiplying `1.07` by `1000`, seven times over
var a = 1.07 * 1000 * 1000 * 1000 * 1000 * 1000 * 1000 * 1000;

// seven times three digits => 21 digits
a.toString(); // "1.07e21"
```

For regular objects, unless you specify your own, the default toString() (located in Object.prototype.toString()) will return the *internal* [[Class]] (see Chapter 3), like for instance "[object Object]".

But as shown earlier, if an object has its own toString() method on it, and you use that object in a string-like way, its toString() will automatically be called, and the string result of that call will be used instead.

 The way an object is coerced to a string technically goes through the ToPrimitive abstract operation (ES5 spec, section 9.1), but those nuanced details are covered in more detail in the ToNumber section later in this chapter, so we will skip over them here.

Arrays have an overridden default toString() that stringifies as the (string) concatenation of all its values (each stringified themselves), with "," in between each value:

```
var a = [1,2,3];

a.toString(); // "1,2,3"
```

Again, toString() can either be called explicitly, or it will automatically be called if a non-string is used in a string context.

JSON stringification

Another task that seems awfully related to ToString is when you use the JSON.stringify(..) utility to serialize a value to a JSON-compatible string value.

It's important to note that this stringification is not exactly the same thing as coercion. But since it's related to the ToString rules above, we'll take a slight diversion to cover JSON stringification behaviors here.

For most simple values, JSON stringification behaves basically the same as toString() conversions, except that the serialization result is *always a* string:

```
JSON.stringify( 42 );    // "42"
JSON.stringify( "42" );  // ""42"" (a string with a
                         // quoted string value in it)
JSON.stringify( null );  // "null"
JSON.stringify( true );  // "true"
```

Any *JSON-safe* value can be stringified by JSON.stringify(..). But what is *JSON-safe?* Any value that can be represented validly in a JSON representation.

It may be easier to consider values that are *not* JSON-safe. Some examples are undefineds, functions, (ES6+) symbols, and objects with circular references (where property references in an object structure create a never-ending cycle through each other). These are all illegal values for a standard JSON structure, mostly because they aren't portable to other languages that consume JSON values.

The JSON.stringify(..) utility will automatically omit undefined, function, and symbol values when it comes across them. If such a value is found in an array, that value is replaced by null (so that the array position information isn't altered). If found as a property of an object, that property will simply be excluded.

Consider:

```
JSON.stringify( undefined );      // undefined
JSON.stringify( function(){} );   // undefined

JSON.stringify(
   [1,undefined,function(){},4]
);                                // "[1,null,null,4]"
JSON.stringify(
   { a:2, b:function(){} }
);                                // "{"a":2}"
```

But if you try to JSON.stringify(..) an object with circular reference(s) in it, an error will be thrown.

JSON stringification has the special behavior that if an `object` value has a `toJSON()` method defined, this method will be called first to get a value to use for serialization.

If you intend to JSON stringify an object that may contain illegal JSON value(s), or if you just have values in the `object` that aren't appropriate for the serialization, you should define a `toJSON()` method for it that returns a *JSON-safe* version of the `object`.

For example:

```
var o = { };

var a = {
    b: 42,
    c: o,
    d: function(){}
};

// create a circular reference inside `a`
o.e = a;

// would throw an error on the circular reference
// JSON.stringify( a );

// define a custom JSON value serialization
a.toJSON = function() {
    // only include the `b` property for serialization
    return { b: this.b };
};

JSON.stringify( a ); // "{"b":42}"
```

It's a very common misconception that `toJSON()` should return a JSON stringification representation. That's probably incorrect, unless you're wanting to actually stringify the `string` itself (usually not!). `toJSON()` should return the actual regular value (of whatever type) that's appropriate, and `JSON.stringify(..)` itself will handle the stringification.

In other words, `toJSON()` should be interpreted as "to a JSON-safe value suitable for stringification," not "to a JSON string" as many developers mistakenly assume.

Consider:

```
var a = {
    val: [1,2,3],

    // probably correct!
    toJSON: function(){
        return this.val.slice( 1 );
    }
};

var b = {
    val: [1,2,3],

    // probably incorrect!
    toJSON: function(){
        return "[" +
            this.val.slice( 1 ).join() +
            "]";
    }
};

JSON.stringify( a ); // "[2,3]"

JSON.stringify( b ); // ""[2,3]""
```

In the second call, we stringified the returned `string` rather than the `array` itself, which was probably not what we wanted to do.

While we're talking about `JSON.stringify(..)`, let's discuss some lesser-known functionalities that can still be very useful.

An optional second argument can be passed to `JSON.string ify(..)` that is called *replacer*. This argument can either be an `array` or a `function`. It's used to customize the recursive serialization of an `object` by providing a filtering mechanism for which properties should and should not be included, in a similar way to how `toJSON()` can prepare a value for serialization.

If *replacer* is an `array`, it should be an `array` of `strings`, each of which will specify a property name that is allowed to be included in the serialization of the `object`. If a property exists that isn't in this list, it will be skipped.

If *replacer* is a `function`, it will be called once for the `object` itself, and then once for each property in the `object`, and each time is passed two arguments, *key* and *value*. To skip a *key* in the serialization, return `undefined`. Otherwise, return the *value* provided.

```
var a = {
    b: 42,
    c: "42",
    d: [1,2,3]
};

JSON.stringify( a, ["b","c"] ); // "{"b":42,"c":"42"}"

JSON.stringify( a, function(k,v){
    if (k !== "c") return v;
} );
// "{"b":42,"d":[1,2,3]}"
```

 In the function *replacer* case, the key argument
k is undefined for the first call (where the a
object itself is being passed in). The if statement
filters out the property named "c". Stringification is recursive, so the [1,2,3] array has each
of its values (1, 2, and 3) passed as v to *replacer*,
with indexes (0, 1, and 2) as k.

A third optional argument can also be passed to JSON.string
ify(..), called *space*, which is used as indentation for prettier
human-friendly output. *space* can be a positive integer to indicate
how many space characters should be used at each indentation level.
Or, *space* can be a string, in which case up to the first 10 characters
of its value will be used for each indentation level:

```
var a = {
    b: 42,
    c: "42",
    d: [1,2,3]
};

JSON.stringify( a, null, 3 );
// "{
//     "b": 42,
//     "c": "42",
//     "d": [
//         1,
//         2,
//         3
//     ]
// }"

JSON.stringify( a, null, "-----" );
// "{
// -----"b": 42,
```

```
// -----"c": "42",
// -----"d": [
// ----------1,
// ----------2,
// ----------3
// -----]
// }"
```

Remember, JSON.stringify(..) is not directly a form of coercion. We covered it here, however, for two reasons that relate its behavior to ToString coercion:

1. string, number, boolean, and null values all stringify for JSON basically the same as how they coerce to string values via the rules of the ToString abstract operation.

2. If you pass an object value to JSON.stringify(..), and that object has a toJSON() method on it, toJSON() is automatically called to (sort of) "coerce" the value to be *JSON-safe* before stringification.

ToNumber

If any non-number value is used in a way that requires it to be a number, such as a mathematical operation, the ES5 spec defines the ToNumber abstract operation in section 9.3.

For example, true becomes 1 and false becomes 0. undefined becomes NaN, but (curiously) null becomes 0.

ToNumber for a string value essentially works for the most part like the rules/syntax for numeric literals (see Chapter 3). If it fails, the result is NaN (instead of a syntax error as with number literals). One difference is that 0-prefixed octal numbers are not handled as octals (just as normal base-10 decimals) in this operation, though such octals are valid as number literals (see Chapter 2).

The differences between number literal grammar and ToNumber on a string value are subtle and highly nuanced, and thus will not be covered further here. Consult section 9.3.1 of the ES5 spec for more information.

Objects (and arrays) will first be converted to their primitive value equivalent, and the resulting value (if a primitive but not already a number) is coerced to a number according to the ToNumber rules just mentioned.

To convert to this primitive value equivalent, the ToPrimitive abstract operation (ES5 spec, section 9.1) will consult the value in question (using the internal DefaultValue operation—ES5 spec, section 8.12.8) to see if it has a valueOf() method. If valueOf() is available and it returns a primitive value, *that* value is used for the coercion. If not, toString() will provide the value for the coercion, if present.

If neither operation can provide a primitive value, a TypeError is thrown.

As of ES5, you can create such a noncoercible object—one without valueOf() and toString()—if it has a null value for its [[Proto type]], typically created with Object.create(null). See the *this & Object Prototypes* title in this series for more information on [[Pro totype]]s.

 We cover how to coerce to numbers later in this chapter in detail, but for this next code snippet, just assume the Number(..) function does so.

Consider:

```
var a = {
    valueOf: function(){
        return "42";
    }
};

var b = {
    toString: function(){
        return "42";
    }
};

var c = [4,2];
c.toString = function(){
    return this.join( "" ); // "42"
};
```

```
Number( a );                // 42
Number( b );                // 42
Number( c );                // 42
Number( "" );               // 0
Number( [] );               // 0
Number( [ "abc" ] );        // NaN
```

ToBoolean

Next, let's have a little chat about how booleans behave in JS. There's lots of confusion and misconception floating out there around this topic, so pay close attention!

First and foremost, JS has actual keywords `true` and `false`, and they behave exactly as you'd expect of boolean values. It's a common misconception that the values `1` and `0` are identical to `true`/`false`. While that may be true in other languages, in JS the numbers are numbers and the booleans are booleans. You can coerce `1` to `true` (and vice versa) or `0` to `false` (and vice versa). But they're not the same.

Falsy values

But that's not the end of the story. We need to discuss how values other than the two booleans behave whenever you coerce *to* their boolean equivalent.

All of JavaScript's values can be divided into two categories:

1. Values that will become `false` if coerced to `boolean`
2. Everything else (which will obviously become `true`)

I'm not just being facetious. The JS spec defines a specific, narrow list of values that will coerce to `false` when coerced to a `boolean` value.

How do we know what the list of values is? In the ES5 spec, section 9.2 defines a `ToBoolean` abstract operation, which says exactly what happens for all the possible values when you try to coerce them "to boolean."

From that table, we get the following as the so-called "falsy" values list:

- `undefined`
- `null`

- `false`
- `+0`, `-0`, and `NaN`
- `""`

That's it. If a value is on that list, it's a "falsy" value, and it will coerce to `false` if you force a `boolean` coercion on it.

By logical conclusion, if a value is *not* on that list, it must be on *another list*, which we call the "truthy" values list. But JS doesn't really define a "truthy" list per se. It gives some examples, such as saying explicitly that all objects are truthy, but mostly the spec just implies that *anything not explicitly on the falsy list is therefore truthy.*

Falsy objects

Wait a minute, that section title even sounds contradictory. I literally *just said* the spec calls all objects truthy, right? There should be no such thing as a "falsy object."

What could that possibly even mean?

You might be tempted to think it means an object wrapper (see Chapter 3) around a falsy value (such as `""`, `0`, or `false`). But don't fall into that *trap*.

That's a subtle specification joke some of you may get.

Consider:

```
var a = new Boolean( false );
var b = new Number( 0 );
var c = new String( "" );
```

We know all three values here are objects (see Chapter 3) wrapped around obviously falsy values. But do these objects behave as `true` or as `false`? That's easy to answer:

```
var d = Boolean( a && b && c );

d; // true
```

So, all three behave as `true`, as that's the only way d could end up as `true`.

 Notice the way the `Boolean( .. )` wrapped around the `a && b && c` expression—you might wonder why that's there. We'll come back to that later in this chapter, so make a mental note of it. For a sneak peek (trivia-wise), try for yourself what d will be if you just do `d = a && b && c` without the `Boolean(..)` call!

So, if "falsy objects" are not just objects wrapped around falsy values, what the heck are they?

The tricky part is that they can show up in your JS program, but they're not actually part of JavaScript itself.

What!?

There are certain cases where browsers have created their own sort of *exotic* values behavior, namely this idea of "falsy objects," on top of regular JS semantics.

A "falsy object" is a value that looks and acts like a normal object (properties, etc.), but when you coerce it to a `boolean`, it coerces to a `false` value.

Why!?

The most well-known case is `document.all`, an array-like (object) provided to your JS program *by the DOM* (not the JS engine itself), which exposes elements in your page to your JS program. It *used* to behave like a normal object—it would act truthy. But not anymore.

`document.all` itself was never really "standard" and has long since been deprecated/abandoned.

"Can't they just remove it, then?" Sorry, nice try. Wish they could. But there's far too many legacy JS code bases out there that rely on using it.

So, why make it act falsy? Because coercions of `document.all` to `boolean` (like in `if` statements) were almost always used as a means of detecting old, nonstandard IE. IE has long since come up to standards compliance, and in many cases is pushing the Web forward as much or more than any other browser.

But all that old if (document.all) { /* it's IE */ } code is still out there, and much of it is probably never going away. All this legacy code is still assuming it's running in decade-old IE, which just leads to a bad browsing experience for IE users.

So, we can't remove document.all completely, but IE doesn't want if (document.all) { .. } code to work anymore, so that users in modern IE get new, standards-compliant code logic.

"What should we do?"

"I've got it! Let's bastardize the JS type system and pretend that docu ment.all is falsy!"

Ugh. That sucks. It's a crazy gotcha that most JS developers don't understand. But the alternative (doing nothing about the above no-win problems) sucks *just a little bit more.*

So... that's what we've got: crazy, nonstandard "falsy objects" added to JavaScript by the browsers. Yay!

Truthy values

Back to the truthy list. What exactly are the truthy values? Remember: a value is truthy if it's not on the falsy list.

Consider:

```
var a = "false";
var b = "0";
var c = "'";

var d = Boolean( a && b && c );

d;
```

What value do you expect d to have here? It's gotta be either true or false.

It's true. Why? Because despite the contents of those string values looking like falsy values, the string values themselves are all truthy, because "" is the only string value on the falsy list.

What about these?

```
var a = [];              // empty array--truthy or falsy?
var b = {};              // empty object--truthy or falsy?
var c = function(){};    // empty function--truthy or falsy?
```

```
var d = Boolean( a && b && c );

d;
```

Yep, you guessed it, d is still `true` here. Why? Same reason as before. Despite what it may seem like, [ ], { }, and `function(){}` are *not* on the falsy list, and thus are truthy values.

In other words, the truthy list is infinitely long. It's impossible to make such a list. You can only make a finite falsy list and consult *it*.

Take five minutes, write the falsy list on a Post-it note for your computer monitor, or memorize it if you prefer. Either way, you'll easily be able to construct a virtual truthy list whenever you need it by simply asking if it's on the falsy list or not.

The importance of truthy and falsy is in understanding how a value will behave if you coerce it (either explicitly or implicitly) to a `boolean` value. Now that you have those two lists in mind, we can dive into coercion examples themselves.

Explicit Coercion

Explicit coercion refers to type conversions that are obvious and explicit. There's a wide range of type conversion usage that clearly falls under the *explicit* coercion category for most developers.

The goal here is to identify patterns in our code where we can make it clear and obvious that we're converting a value from one type to another, so as to not leave potholes for future developers to trip into. The more explicit we are, the more likely someone later will be able to read our code and understand without undue effort what our intent was.

It would be hard to find any salient disagreements with *explicit coercion*, as it most closely aligns with how the commonly accepted practice of type conversion works in statically typed languages. As such, we'll take for granted (for now) that *explicit* coercion can be agreed upon to not be evil or controversial. We'll revisit this later, though.

Explicitly: Strings <--> Numbers

We'll start with the simplest and perhaps most common coercion operation: coercing values between `string` and `number` representation.

To coerce between `strings` and `numbers`, we use the built-in `String(..)` and `Number(..)` functions (which we referred to as "native constructors" in Chapter 3), but *very importantly*, we do not use the `new` keyword in front of them. As such, we're not creating object wrappers.

Instead, we're actually *explicitly coercing* between the two types:

```
var a = 42;
var b = String( a );

var c = "3.14";
var d = Number( c );

b; // "42"
d; // 3.14
```

`String(..)` coerces from any other value to a primitive `string` value, using the rules of the `ToString` operation discussed earlier. `Number(..)` coerces from any other value to a primitive `number` value, using the rules of the `ToNumber` operation discussed earlier.

I call this *explicit* coercion because in general, it's pretty obvious to most developers that the end result of these operations is the applicable type conversion.

In fact, this usage actually looks a lot like it does in some other statically typed languages.

For example, in C/C++, you can say either `(int)x` or `int(x)`, and both will convert the value in x to an integer. Both forms are valid, but many prefer the latter, which kinda looks like a function call. In JavaScript, when you say `Number(x)`, it looks awfully similar. Does it matter that it's *actually* a function call in JS? Not really.

Besides `String(..)` and `Number(..)`, there are other ways to "explicitly" convert these values between `string` and `number`:

```
var a = 42;
var b = a.toString();

var c = "3.14";
```

```
var d = +c;

b; // "42"
d; // 3.14
```

Calling a.toString() is ostensibly explicit (pretty clear that "toString" means "to a string"), but there's some hidden implicitness here. toString() cannot be called on a *primitive* value like 42. So JS automatically "boxes" (see Chapter 3) 42 in an object wrapper, so that toString() can be called against the object. In other words, you might call it "explicitly implicit."

+c here is showing the *unary operator* form (operator with only one operand) of the + operator. Instead of performing mathematic addition (or string concatenation—see below), the unary + explicitly coerces its operand (c) to a number value.

Is +c *explicit* coercion? Depends on your experience and perspective. If you know (which you do, now!) that unary + is explicitly intended for number coercion, then it's pretty explicit and obvious. However, if you've never seen it before, it can seem awfully confusing, implicit, with hidden side effects, etc.

 The generally accepted perspective in the open source JS community is that unary + is an accepted form of *explicit* coercion.

Even if you really like the +c form, there are definitely places where it can look awfully confusing. Consider:

```
var c = "3.14";
var d = 5+ +c;

d; // 8.14
```

The unary - operator also coerces like + does, but it also flips the sign of the number. However, you cannot put two (- -) next to each other to unflip the sign, as that's parsed as the decrement operator. Instead, you would need to do - -"3.14" with a space in between, and that would result in coercion to 3.14.

You can probably dream up all sorts of hideous combinations of binary operators (like + for addition) next to the unary form of an operator. Here's another crazy example:

```
1 + - + + + - + 1;   // 2
```

You should strongly consider avoiding unary + (or -) coercion when it's immediately adjacent to other operators. While the above works, it would almost universally be considered a bad idea. Even d = +c (or d =+ c for that matter!) can far too easily be confused for d += c, which is entirely different!

Another extremely confusing place for unary + to be used adjacent to another operator would be the ++ increment operator and -- decrement operator. For example, consider a +++b, a + ++b, and a + + +b. See "Expression Side Effects" on page 125 for more about ++.

Remember, we're trying to be explicit and *reduce* confusion, not make it much worse!

Date to number

Another common usage of the unary + operator is to coerce a Date object into a number, because the result is the Unix timestamp (milliseconds elapsed since 1 January 1970 00:00:00 UTC) representation of the date/time value:

```
var d = new Date( "Mon, 18 Aug 2014 08:53:06 CDT" );

+d; // 1408369986000
```

The most common usage of this idiom is to get the current *now* moment as a timestamp, such as:

```
var timestamp = +new Date();
```

Some developers are aware of a peculiar syntactic "trick" in JavaScript, which is that the () set on a constructor call (a function called with new) is *optional* only if there are no arguments to pass. So you may run across the var timestamp = +new Date; form. However, not all developers agree that omitting the () improves readability, as it's an uncommon syntax exception that only applies to the new fn() call form and not the regular fn() call form.

But coercion is not the only way to get the timestamp out of a `Date` object. A noncoercion approach is perhaps even preferable, as it's even more explicit:

```
var timestamp = new Date().getTime();
// var timestamp = (new Date()).getTime();
// var timestamp = (new Date).getTime();
```

But an *even more* preferable noncoercion option is to use the `Date.now()` static function added in ES5:

```
var timestamp = Date.now();
```

And if you want to polyfill `Date.now()` into older browsers, it's pretty simple:

```
if (!Date.now) {
    Date.now = function() {
        return +new Date();
    };
}
```

I'd recommend skipping the coercion forms related to dates. Use `Date.now()` for current *now* timestamps, and `new Date( .. ).get Time()` for getting a timestamp of a specific *non-now* date/time that you need to specify.

The curious case of the ~

One coercive JS operator that is often overlooked and usually very confused is the tilde ~ operator (aka "bitwise NOT"). Many of those who even understand what it does will often still want to avoid it. But sticking to the spirit of our approach in this book and series, let's dig into it to find out if ~ has anything useful to give us.

In "32-Bit (Signed) Integers" on page 23, we covered how bitwise operators in JS are defined only for 32-bit operations, which means they force their operands to conform to 32-bit value representations. The rules for how this happens are controlled by the `ToInt32` abstract operation (ES5 spec, section 9.5).

`ToInt32` first does a `ToNumber` coercion, which means if the value is `"123"`, it's going to first become `123` before the `ToInt32` rules are applied.

While not *technically* coercion itself (since the type doesn't change!), using bitwise operators (like | or ~) with certain special number values produces a coercive effect that results in a different `number` value.

For example, let's first consider the | "bitwise OR" operator used in the otherwise no-op idiom 0 | x, which (as Chapter 2 showed) essentially only does the `ToInt32` conversion:

```
0 | -0;        // 0
0 | NaN;       // 0
0 | Infinity;  // 0
0 | -Infinity; // 0
```

These special numbers aren't 32-bit representable (since they come from the 64-bit IEEE 754 standard—see Chapter 2), so `ToInt32` just specifies 0 as the result from these values.

It's debatable if 0 | __ is an *explicit* form of this coercive `ToInt32` operation or if it's more *implicit*. From the spec perspective, it's unquestionably *explicit*, but if you don't understand bitwise operations at this level, it can seem a bit more *implicitly* magical. Nevertheless, consistent with other assertions in this chapter, we will call it *explicit*.

So, let's turn our attention back to ~. The ~ operator first "coerces" to a 32-bit `number` value, and then performs a bitwise negation (flipping each bit's parity).

 This is very similar to how ! not only coerces its value to `boolean` but also flips its parity (see the discussion of the "unary !" operator in "Explicitly: * --> Boolean" on page 83).

But... what!? Why do we care about bits being flipped? That's some pretty specialized, nuanced stuff. It's pretty rare for JS developers to need to reason about individual bits.

Another way of thinking about the definition of ~ comes from old-school computer science/discrete mathematics: ~ performs two's complement. Great, thanks, that's totally clearer!

Let's try again: ~x is roughly the same as -(x+1). That's weird, but slightly easier to reason about. So:

```
~42;   // -(42+1) ==> -43
```

You're probably still wondering what the heck all this ~ stuff is about, or why it really matters for a coercion discussion. Let's quickly get to the point.

Consider -(x+1). What's the only value that can you can perform that operation on that will produce a 0 (or -0 technically!) result? -1. In other words, ~ used with a range of number values will produce a falsy (easily coercible to false) 0 value for the -1 input value, and any other truthy number otherwise.

Why is that relevant?

-1 is commonly called a "sentinel value," which basically means a value that's given an arbitrary semantic meaning within the greater set of values of its same type (numbers). The C-language uses -1 sentinel values for many functions that return >= 0 values for "success" and -1 for "failure."

JavaScript adopted this precedent when defining the string operation indexOf(..), which searches for a substring and if found returns its zero-based index position, or -1 if not found.

It's pretty common to try to use indexOf(..) not just as an operation to get the position, but as a boolean check of presence/absence of a substring in another string. Here's how developers usually perform such checks:

```
var a = "Hello World";

if (a.indexOf( "lo" ) >= 0) {   // true
    // found it!
}
if (a.indexOf( "lo" ) != -1) {  // true
    // found it
}

if (a.indexOf( "ol" ) < 0) {    // true
    // not found!
}
if (a.indexOf( "ol" ) == -1) {  // true
    // not found!
}
```

I find it kind of gross to look at >= 0 or == -1. It's basically a "leaky abstraction," in that it's leaking underlying implementation behavior —the usage of sentinel -1 for "failure"—into my code. I would prefer to hide such a detail.

And now, finally, we see why ~ could help us! Using ~ with indexOf() "coerces" (actually just transforms) the value to be appropriately boolean-coercible:

```
var a = "Hello World";

~a.indexOf( "lo" );        // -4   <-- truthy!

if (~a.indexOf( "lo" )) {  // true
    // found it!
}

~a.indexOf( "ol" );        // 0    <-- falsy!
!~a.indexOf( "ol" );       // true

if (!~a.indexOf( "ol" )) { // true
    // not found!
}
```

~ takes the return value of indexOf(..) and transforms it: for the "failure" -1 we get the falsy 0, and every other value is truthy.

 The -(x+1) pseudo-algorithm for ~ would imply that ~-1 is -0, but actually it produces 0 because the underlying operation is bitwise, not mathematic.

Technically, if (~a.indexOf(..)) is still relying on *implicit* coercion of its resultant 0 to false or nonzero to true. But overall, ~ still feels to me more like an *explicit* coercion mechanism, as long as you know what it's intended to do in this idiom.

I find this to be cleaner code than the previous >= 0 / == -1 clutter.

Truncating bits

There's one more place ~ may show up in code you run accross: some developers use the double tilde ~~ to truncate the decimal part of a number (i.e., "coerce" it to a whole number integer). It's commonly (though mistakenly) said that this is the same result as calling Math.floor(..).

How ~~ works is that the first ~ applies the ToInt32 "coercion" and does the bitwise flip, and then the second ~ does another bitwise flip, flipping all the bits back to the original state. The end result is just the ToInt32 "coercion" (aka truncation).

The bitwise double-flip of ~~ is very similar to the parity double-negate !! behavior, explained in "Explicitly: * --> Boolean" on page 83.

However, ~~ needs some caution/clarification. First, it only works reliably on 32-bit values. But more importantly, it doesn't work the same on negative numbers as Math.floor(..) does!

```
Math.floor( -49.6 );    // -50
~~-49.6;                // -49
```

Setting the Math.floor(..) difference aside, ~~x can truncate to a (32-bit) integer. But so does x | 0, and seemingly with (slightly) *less effort*.

So, why might you choose ~~x over x | 0, then? Operator precedence (see Chapter 5):

```
~~1E20 / 10;         // 166199296

1E20 | 0 / 10;       // 1661992960
(1E20 | 0) / 10;     // 166199296
```

Just as with all other advice here, use ~ and ~~ as explicit mechanisms for "coercion" and value transformation only if everyone who reads/writes such code is properly aware of how these operators work!

Explicitly: Parsing Numeric Strings

A similar outcome to coercing a string to a number can be achieved by parsing a number out of a string's character contents. There are, however, distinct differences between this parsing and the type conversion we examined above.

Consider:

```
var a = "42";
var b = "42px";

Number( a );    // 42
parseInt( a );  // 42

Number( b );    // NaN
parseInt( b );  // 42
```

Parsing a numeric value out of a string is *tolerant* of non-numeric characters—it just stops parsing left-to-right when encountered—whereas coercion is *not tolerant* and fails, resulting in the NaN value.

Parsing should not be seen as a substitute for coercion. These two tasks, while similar, have different purposes. Parse a string as a num ber when you don't know/care what other non-numeric characters there may be on the right-hand side. Coerce a string (to a number) when the only acceptable values are numeric and something like "42px" should be rejected as a number.

> parseInt(..) has a twin, parseFloat(..), which (as it sounds) pulls out a floating-point number from a string.

Don't forget that parseInt(..) operates on string values. It makes absolutely no sense to pass a number value to parseInt(..). Nor would it make sense to pass any other type of value, like true, func tion(){..}, or [1,2,3].

If you pass a non-string, the value you pass will automatically be coerced to a string first (see "ToString" on page 59), which would clearly be a kind of hidden *implicit* coercion. It's a really bad idea to rely upon such behavior in your program, so never use par seInt(..) with a non-string value.

Prior to ES5, another gotcha existed with parseInt(..), which was the source of many JS programs' bugs. If you didn't pass a second argument to indicate which numeric base (aka radix) to use for interpreting the numeric string contents, parseInt(..) would look at the first character to make a guess.

If the first character was x or X, the guess (by convention) was that you wanted to interpret the string as a hexadecimal (base-16) num ber. If the first character was 0, the guess (again, by convention) was that you wanted to interpret the string as an octal (base-8) number.

Hexadecimal strings (with the leading x or X) aren't terribly easy to get mixed up. But the octal number guessing proved devilishly com mon. For example:

```
var hour = parseInt( selectedHour.value );
var minute = parseInt( selectedMinute.value );

console.log(
   "The time you selected was: " + hour + ":" + minute
);
```

Seems harmless, right? Try selecting 08 for the hour and 09 for the minute. You'll get 0:0. Why? because neither 8 nor 9 are valid characters in octal base-8.

The pre-ES5 fix was simple, but so easy to forget: *always pass 10 as the second argument*. This was totally safe:

```
var hour = parseInt( selectedHour.value, 10 );
var minute = parseInt( selectedMiniute.value, 10 );
```

As of ES5, parseInt(..) no longer guesses. Unless you say otherwise, it assumes base-10. That's much nicer. Just be careful if your code has to run in pre-ES5 environments, in which case you still need to pass 10 for the radix.

Parsing non-strings

One somewhat infamous example of parseInt(..)'s behavior is highlighted in a sarcastic joke post a few years ago, poking fun at this JS behavior:

```
parseInt( 1/0, 19 ); // 18
```

The assumptive (but totally invalid) assertion was, "If I pass in Infinity, and parse an integer out of that, I should get Infinity back, not 18." Surely, JS must be crazy for this outcome, right?

Though this example is obviously contrived and unreal, let's indulge the madness for a moment and examine whether JS really is that crazy.

First off, the most obvious sin committed here is to pass a non-string to parseInt(..). That's a no-no. Do it and you're asking for trouble. But even if you do, JS politely coerces what you pass in into a string that it can try to parse.

Some would argue that this is unreasonable behavior, and that par seInt(..) should refuse to operate on a non-string value. Should it perhaps throw an error? That would be very Java-like, frankly. I shudder at thinking JS should start throwing errors all over the place so that try..catch is needed around almost every line.

Should it return NaN? Maybe. But...what about:

```
parseInt( new String( "42") );
```

Should that fail, too? It's a non-string value. If you want that String object wrapper to be unboxed to "42", then is it really so unusual for 42 to first become "42" so that 42 can be parsed back out?

I would argue that this half-*explicit*, half-*implicit* coercion that can occur can often be a very helpful thing. For example:

```
var a = {
    num: 21,
    toString: function() { return String( this.num * 2 ); }
};

parseInt( a ); // 42
```

The fact that parseInt(..) forcibly coerces its value to a string to perform the parse on is quite sensible. If you pass in garbage, and you get garbage back out, don't blame the trash can—it just did its job faithfully.

So, if you pass in a value like Infinity (the result of 1 / 0 obviously), what sort of string representation would make the most sense for its coercion? Only two reasonable choices come to mind: "Infinity" and "∞". JS chose "Infinity". I'm glad it did.

I think it's a good thing that all values in JS have some sort of default string representation, so that they aren't mysterious black boxes that we can't debug and reason about.

Now, what about base-19? Obviously, completely bogus and contrived. No real JS programs use base-19. It's absurd. But again, let's indulge the ridiulousness. In base-19, the valid numeric characters are 0 - 9 and a - i (case insensitive).

So, back to our parseInt(1/0, 19) example. It's essentially par seInt("Infinity", 19). How does it parse? The first character is "I", which is value 18 in the silly base-19. The second character "n" is not in the valid set of numeric characters, and as such the parsing simply politely stops, just like when it ran across "p" in "42px".

The result? 18. Exactly like it sensibly should be. The behaviors involved to get us there, and not to an error or to Infinity itself, are *very important* to JS, and should not be so easily discarded.

Other examples of this behavior with parseInt(..) that may be surprising but are quite sensible include:

```
parseInt( 0.000008 );        // 0   ("0" from "0.000008")
parseInt( 0.0000008 );       // 8   ("8" from "8e-7")
parseInt( false, 16 );       // 250 ("fa" from "false")
parseInt( parseInt, 16 );    // 15  ("f" from "function..")

parseInt( "0x10" );          // 16
parseInt( "103", 2 );        // 2
```

parseInt(..) is actually pretty predictable and consistent in its behavior. If you use it correctly, you'll get sensible results. If you use it incorrectly, the crazy results you get are not the fault of JavaScript.

Explicitly: * --> Boolean

Now, let's examine coercing from any non-boolean value to a boolean.

Just like with String(..) and Number(..) above, Boolean(..) (without the new, of course!) is an explicit way of forcing the ToBoolean coercion:

```
var a = "0";
var b = [];
var c = {};

var d = "";
var e = 0;
var f = null;
var g;

Boolean( a ); // true
Boolean( b ); // true
Boolean( c ); // true

Boolean( d ); // false
Boolean( e ); // false
Boolean( f ); // false
Boolean( g ); // false
```

While Boolean(..) is clearly explicit, it's not at all common or idiomatic.

Just like the unary + operator coerces a value to a number (see above), the unary ! negate operator explicitly coerces a value to a boolean. The *problem* is that it also flips the value from truthy to falsy or vice versa. So, the most common way JS developers explicitly coerce to `boolean` is to use the `!!` double-negate operator, because the second `!` will flip the parity back to the original:

```
var a = "0";
var b = [];
var c = {};

var d = "";
var e = 0;
var f = null;
var g;

!!a;    // true
!!b;    // true
!!c;    // true

!!d;    // false
!!e;    // false
!!f;    // false
!!g;    // false
```

Any of these `ToBoolean` coercions would happen *implicitly* without the `Boolean(..)` or `!!`, if used in a `boolean` context such as an `if (..)` .. statement. But the goal here is to explicitly force the value to a `boolean` to make it clearer that the `ToBoolean` coercion is intended.

Another example use case for explicit `ToBoolean` coercion is if you want to force a `true`/`false` value coercion in the JSON serialization of a data structure:

```
var a = [
    1,
    function(){ /*..*/ },
    2,
    function(){ /*..*/ }
];

JSON.stringify( a ); // "[1,null,2,null]"

JSON.stringify( a, function(key,val){
    if (typeof val == "function") {
        // force `ToBoolean` coercion of the function
        return !!val;
    }
    else {
        return val;
    }
} );
// "[1,true,2,true]"
```

If you come to JavaScript from Java, you may recognize this idiom:

```
var a = 42;

var b = a ? true : false;
```

The ? : ternary operator will test a for truthiness, and based on that test will either assign true or false to b, accordingly.

On its surface, this idiom looks like a form of *explicit* ToBoolean-type coercion, since it's obvious that only either true or false come out of the operation.

However, there's a hidden *implicit* coercion, in that the a expression has to first be coerced to boolean to perform the truthiness test. I'd call this idiom "explicitly implicit." Furthermore, I'd suggest you should avoid this idiom completely in JavaScript. It offers no real benefit, and worse, masquerades as something it's not.

Boolean(a) and !!a are far better as *explicit* coercion options.

Implicit Coercion

Implicit coercion refers to type conversions that are hidden, with nonobvious side effects that implicitly occur from other actions. In other words, *implicit* coercions are any type conversions that aren't obvious (to you).

While it's clear what the goal of *explicit* coercion is (making code explicit and more understandable), it might be *too* obvious that *implicit* coercion has the opposite goal: making code harder to understand.

Taken at face value, I believe that's where much of the ire towards coercion comes from. The majority of complaints about "JavaScript coercion" are actually aimed (whether they realize it or not) at *implicit* coercion.

Douglas Crockford, author of *JavaScript: The Good Parts*, has claimed in many conference talks and writings that JavaScript coercion should be avoided. But what he seems to mean is that *implicit* coercion is bad (in his opinion). However, if you read his own code, you'll find plenty of examples of coercion, both *implicit* and *explicit*! In truth, his angst seems to primarily be directed at the == operation, but as you'll see in this chapter, that's only part of the coercion mechanism.

So, is implicit coercion evil? Is it dangerous? Is it a flaw in JavaScript's design? Should we avoid it at all costs?

I bet most of you readers are inclined to enthusiastically cheer, "Yes!"

Not so fast. Hear me out.

Let's take a different perspective on what *implicit* coercion is, and can be, than just that it's "the opposite of the good explicit kind of coercion." That's far too narrow and misses an important nuance.

Let's define the goal of *implicit* coercion as to reduce verbosity, boilerplate, and/or unnecessary implementation detail that clutters up our code with noise that distracts from the more important intent.

Simplifying Implicitly

Before we even get to JavaScript, let me suggest something pseudo-code'ish from some theoretical strongly typed language to illustrate:

```
SomeType x = SomeType( AnotherType( y ) )
```

In this example, I have some arbitrary type of value in y that I want to convert to the SomeType type. The problem is, this language can't go directly from whatever y currently is to SomeType. It needs an intermediate step, where it first converts to AnotherType, and then from AnotherType to SomeType.

Now, what if that language (or definition you could create yourself with the language) *did* just let you say:

```
SomeType x = SomeType( y )
```

Wouldn't you generally agree that we simplified the type conversion here to reduce the unnecessary "noise" of the intermediate conversion step? I mean, is it *really* all that important, right here at this point in the code, to see and deal with the fact that y goes to Another Type first before then going to SomeType?

Some would argue, at least in some circumstances, yes. But I think an equal argument can be made of many other circumstances that here, the simplification *actually aids in the readability of the code* by abstracting or hiding away such details, either in the language itself or in our own abstractions.

Undoubtedly, behind the scenes, somewhere, the intermediate conversion step is still happening. But if that detail is hidden from view here, we can just reason about getting y to type SomeType as an generic operation and hide the messy details.

While not a perfect analogy, what I'm going to argue throughout the rest of this chapter is that JS *implicit* coercion can be thought of as providing a similar aid to your code.

But, and this is very important, that is not an unbounded, absolute statement. There are definitely plenty of *evils* lurking around *implicit* coercion that will harm your code much more than any potential readability improvements. Clearly, we have to learn how to avoid such constructs so we don't poison our code with all manner of bugs.

Many developers believe that if a mechanism can do some useful thing *A* but can also be abused or misused to do some awful thing *Z*, then we should throw out that mechanism altogether, just to be safe.

My encouragement to you is: don't settle for that. Don't "throw the baby out with the bathwater." Don't assume *implicit* coercion is all bad because all you think you've ever seen is its "bad parts." I think there are "good parts" here, and I want to help and inspire more of you to find and embrace them!

Implicitly: Strings <--> Numbers

Earlier in this chapter, we explored *explicitly* coercing between string and number values. Now, let's explore the same task but with *implicit* coercion approaches. But before we do, we have to examine some nuances of operations that will *implicitly* force coercion.

The + operator is overloaded to serve the purposes of both number addition and string concatenation. So how does JS know which type of operation you want to use? Consider:

```
var a = "42";
var b = "0";

var c = 42;
var d = 0;

a + b; // "420"
c + d; // 42
```

What's different that causes "420" versus 42? It's a common misconception that the difference is whether one or both of the operands is a string, as that means + will assume string concatenation. While that's partially true, it's more complicated than that.

Consider:

```
var a = [1,2];
var b = [3,4];

a + b; // "1,23,4"
```

Neither of these operands is a string, but clearly they were both coerced to strings and then the string concatenation kicked in. So what's really going on?

 Deeply nitty gritty spec-speak coming, so skip the next two paragraphs if that intimidates you!

According to the ES5 spec, section 11.6.1, the + algorithm (when an object value is an operand) will concatenate if either operand is either already a string, or if the following steps produce a string representation. So, when + receives an object (including array) for either operand, it first calls the ToPrimitive abstract operation (section 9.1) on the value, which then calls the [[DefaultValue]] algorithm (section 8.12.8) with a context hint of number.

If you're paying close attention, you'll notice that this operation is now identical to how the ToNumber abstract operation handles objects (see "ToNumber" on page 65). The valueOf() operation on the `array` will fail to produce a simple primitive, so it then falls to a `toString()` representation. The two `array`s thus become `"1,2"` and `"3,4"`, respectively. Now, `+` concatenates the two `string`s as you'd normally expect: `"1,23,4"`.

Let's set aside those messy details and go back to an earlier, simplified explanation: if either operand to `+` is a `string` (or become one with the above steps!), the operation will be `string` concatenation. Otherwise, it's always numeric addition.

 A commonly cited coercion gotcha is `[] + {}` versus `{} + []`, as those two expressions result, respectively, in `"[object Object]"` and `0`. There's more to it, though, and we cover those details in "Blocks" on page 134.

What's that mean for *implicit* coercion?

You can coerce a `number` to a `string` simply by "adding" the `number` and the `""` empty `string`:

```
var a = 42;
var b = a + "";

b; // "42"
```

 Numeric addition with the `+` operator is commutative, which means `2 + 3` is the same as `3 + 2`. String concatenation with `+` is obviously not generally commutative, *but* with the specific case of `""`, it's effectively commutative, as `a + ""` and `"" + a` will produce the same result.

It's extremely common/idiomatic to (*implicitly*) coerce `number` to `string` with a `+ ""` operation. In fact, interestingly, even some of the most vocal crticics of *implicit* coercion still use that approach in their own code, instead of one of its *explicit* alternatives.

I think this is a great example of a useful form in *implicit coercion*, despite how frequently the mechanism gets criticized!

Comparing this *implicit* coercion of `a + ""` to our earlier example of `String(a)` *explicit* coercion, there's one additional quirk to be aware of. Because of how the `ToPrimitive` abstract operation works, `a + ""` invokes `valueOf()` on the `a` value, whose return value is then finally converted to a `string` via the internal `ToString` abstract operation. But `String(a)` just invokes `toString()` directly.

Both approaches ultimately result in a `string`, but if you're using an `object` instead of a regular primitive `number` value, you may not necessarily get the *same* `string` value!

Consider:

```
var a = {
    valueOf: function() { return 42; },
    toString: function() { return 4; }
};

a + "";        // "42"

String( a );   // "4"
```

Generally, this sort of gotcha won't bite you unless you're really trying to create confusing data structures and operations, but you should be careful if you're defining both your own `valueOf()` and `toString()` methods for some `object`, as how you coerce the value could affect the outcome.

What about the other direction? How can we *implicitly coerce* from `string` to `number`?

```
var a = "3.14";
var b = a - 0;

b; // 3.14
```

The `-` operator is defined only for numeric subtraction, so `a - 0` forces `a`'s value to be coerced to a `number`. While far less common, `a * 1` or `a / 1` would accomplish the same result, as those operators are also only defined for numeric operations.

What about `object` values with the `-` operator? Similar story as for `+` above:

```
var a = [3];
var b = [1];

a - b; // 2
```

Both `array` values have to become `numbers`, but they end up first being coerced to `strings` (using the expected `toString()` serialization), and then are coerced to numbers, for the - subtraction to perform on.

So, is *implicit* coercion of string and number values the ugly evil you've always heard horror stories about? I don't personally think so.

Compare b = String(a) (*explicit*) to b = a + "" (*implicit*). I think cases can be made for both approaches being useful in your code. Certainly b = a + "" is quite a bit more common in JS programs, proving its own utility regardless of *feelings* about the merits or hazards of *implicit* coercion in general.

Implicitly: Booleans --> Numbers

I think a case where *implicit* coercion can really shine is in simplifying certain types of complicated boolean logic into simple numeric addition. Of course, this is not a general-purpose technique, but a specific solution for specific cases.

Consider:

```
function onlyOne(a,b,c) {
    return !!((a && !b && !c) ||
        (!a && b && !c) || (!a && !b && c));
}

var a = true;
var b = false;

onlyOne( a, b, b ); // true
onlyOne( b, a, b ); // true

onlyOne( a, b, a ); // false
```

This onlyOne(..) utility should only return true if exactly one of the arguments is true / truthy. It's using *implicit* coercion on the truthy checks and *explicit* coercion on the others, including the final return value.

But what if we needed that utility to be able to handle four, five, or twenty flags in the same way? It's pretty difficult to imagine implementing code that would handle all those permutations of comparisons.

But here's where coercing the boolean values to numbers (0 or 1, obviously) can greatly help:

```
function onlyOne() {
    var sum = 0;
    for (var i=0; i < arguments.length; i++) {
        // skip falsy values. same as treating
        // them as 0's, but avoids NaN's.
        if (arguments[i]) {
            sum += arguments[i];
        }
    }
    return sum == 1;
}

var a = true;
var b = false;

onlyOne( b, a );              // true
onlyOne( b, a, b, b, b );     // true

onlyOne( b, b );              // false
onlyOne( b, a, b, b, b, a );  // false
```

 Of course, instead of the for loop in onlyOne(..), you could more tersely use the ES5 reduce(..) utility, but I didn't want to obscure the concepts.

What we're doing here is relying on the 1 for true/truthy coercions, and numerically adding them all up. sum += arguments[i] uses *implicit* coercion to make that happen. If one and only one value in the arguments list is true, then the numeric sum will be 1, otherwise the sum will not be 1 and thus the desired condition is not met.

We could of course do this with *explicit* coercion instead:

```
function onlyOne() {
    var sum = 0;
    for (var i=0; i < arguments.length; i++) {
        sum += Number( !!arguments[i] );
    }
    return sum === 1;
}
```

We first use !!arguments[i] to force the coercion of the value to true or false. That's so you could pass non-boolean values in, like onlyOne("42", 0), and it would still work as expected (otherwise you'd end up with string concatenation and the logic would be incorrect).

Once we're sure it's a `boolean`, we do another *explicit* coercion with `Number(..)` to make sure the value is `0` or `1`.

Is the *explicit* coercion form of this utility "better"? It does avoid the `NaN` trap as explained in the code comments. But, ultimately, it depends on your needs. I personally think the former version, relying on *implicit* coercion, is more elegant (if you won't be passing `undefined` or `NaN`), and the *explicit* version is needlessly more verbose.

But as with almost everything we're discussing here, it's a judgment call.

 Regardless of *implicit* or *explicit* approaches, you could easily make `onlyTwo(..)` or `only Five(..)` variations by simply changing the final comparison from `1`, to `2` or `5`, respectively. That's drastically easier than adding a bunch of `&&` and `||` expressions. So, generally, coercion is very helpful in this case.

Implicitly: * --> Boolean

Now, let's turn our attention to *implicit* coercion to `boolean` values, as it's by far the most common and also by far the most potentially troublesome.

Remember, *implicit* coercion is what kicks in when you use a value in such a way that it forces the value to be converted. For numeric and `string` operations, it's fairly easy to see how the coercions can occur.

But, what sort of expression operations require/force (*implicitly*) a `boolean` coercion?

1. The test expression in an `if (..)` statement

2. The test expression (second clause) in a `for ( .. ; .. ; .. )` header

3. The test expression in `while (..)` and `do..while(..)` loops

4. The test expression (first clause) in `? :` ternary expressions

5. The lefthand operand (which serves as a test expression—see below!) to the || ("logical or") and && ("logical and") operators

Any value used in these contexts that is not already a boolean will be *implicitly* coerced to a boolean using the rules of the ToBoolean abstract operation covered earlier in this chapter.

Let's look at some examples:

```
var a = 42;
var b = "abc";
var c;
var d = null;

if (a) {
    console.log( "yep" );        // yep
}

while (c) {
    console.log( "nope, never runs" );
}

c = d ? a : b;
c;                               // "abc"

if ((a && d) || c) {
    console.log( "yep" );        // yep
}
```

In all these contexts, the non-boolean values are *implicitly coerced* to their boolean equivalents to make the test decisions.

Operators || and &&

It's quite likely that you have seen the || ("logical or") and && ("logical and") operators in most or all other languages you've used. So it'd be natural to assume that they work basically the same in JavaScript as in other similar languages.

There's some very little known, but very important, nuance here.

In fact, I would argue these operators shouldn't even be called "logical ____ operators," as that name is incomplete in describing what they do. If I were to give them a more accurate (if more clumsy) name, I'd call them "selector operators," or more completely, "operand selector operators."

Why? Because they don't actually result in a *logic* value (aka boolean) in JavaScript, as they do in some other languages.

So what *do* they result in? They result in the value of one (and only one) of their two operands. In other words, they select one of the two operand's values.

Quoting the ES5 spec from section 11.11:

> The value produced by a && or || operator is not necessarily of type Boolean. The value produced will always be the value of one of the two operand expressions.

Let's illustrate:

```
var a = 42;
var b = "abc";
var c = null;

a || b;     // 42
a && b;     // "abc"

c || b;     // "abc"
c && b;     // null
```

Wait, what!? Think about that. In languages like C and PHP, those expressions result in true or false, but in JS (and Python and Ruby, for that matter!), the result comes from the values themselves.

Both || and && operators perform a boolean test on the *first operand* (a or c). If the operand is not already boolean (as it's not, here), a normal ToBoolean coercion occurs, so that the test can be performed.

For the || operator, if the test is true, the || expression results in the value of the *first operand* (a or c). If the test is false, the || expression results in the value of the *second operand* (b).

Inversely, for the && operator, if the test is true, the && expression results in the value of the *second operand* (b). If the test is false, the && expression results in the value of the *first operand* (a or c).

The result of a || or && expression is always the underlying value of one of the operands, *not* the (possibly coerced) result of the test. In c && b, c is null, and thus falsy. But the && expression itself results in null (the value in c), not in the coerced false used in the test.

Do you see how these operators act as "operand selectors," now?

Another way of thinking about these operators:

```
a || b;
// roughly equivalent to:
a ? a : b;

a && b;
// roughly equivalent to:
a ? b : a;
```

 I call a || b "roughly equivalent" to a ? a : b because the outcome is identical, but there's a nuanced difference. In a ? a : b, if a was a more complex expression (like for instance one that might have side effects like calling a func tion, etc.), then the a expression would possibly be evaluated twice (if the first evaluation was truthy). By contrast, for a || b, the a expression is evaluated only once, and that value is used both for the coercive test as well as the result value (if appropriate). The same nuance applies to the a && b and a ? b : a expressions.

An extremely common and helpful usage of this behavior, which there's a good chance you may have used before and not fully understood, is:

```
function foo(a,b) {
    a = a || "hello";
    b = b || "world";

    console.log( a + " " + b );
}

foo();                   // "hello world"
foo( "yeah", "yeah!" ); // "yeah yeah!"
```

The a = a || "hello" idiom (sometimes said to be JavaScript's version of the C# "null coallescing operator") acts to test a and if it has no value (or only an undesired falsy value), provides a backup default value ("hello").

Be careful, though!

```
foo( "That's it!", "" ); // "That's it! world" <-- Oops!
```

See the problem? "" as the second argument is a falsy value (see "ToBoolean" on page 67), so the b = b || "world" test fails, and the "world" default value is substituted, even though the intent probably was to have the explicitly passed "" be the value assigned to b.

This || idiom is extremely common, and quite helpful, but you have to use it only in cases where *all falsy values* should be skipped. Otherwise, you'll need to be more explicit in your test, and probably use a ? : ternary instead.

This *default value assignment* idiom is so common (and useful!) that even those who publicly and vehemently decry JavaScript coercion often use it in their own code!

What about &&?

There's another idiom that is quite a bit less commonly authored manually, but which is used by JS minifiers frequently. The && operator "selects" the second operand if and only if the first operand tests as truthy, and this usage is sometimes called the "guard operator" (see also "Short Circuited" on page 140 in Chapter 5)--the first expression test "guards" the second expression:

```
function foo() {
    console.log( a );
}

var a = 42;

a && foo(); // 42
```

foo() gets called only because a tests as truthy. If that test failed, this a && foo() expression statement would just silently stop (sometimes called "short circuiting") and never call foo().

Again, it's not nearly as common for people to author such things. Usually, they'd do if (a) { foo(); } instead. But JS minifiers choose a && foo() because it's much shorter. So, if you ever have to decipher such code, you'll know what it's doing and why.

OK, so || and && have some neat tricks up their sleeve, as long as you're willing to allow the *implicit* coercion into the mix.

Both the a = b || "something" and a && b() idioms rely on short circuiting behavior, which we cover in more detail in "Short Circuited" on page 140 in Chapter 5.

The fact that these operators don't actually result in `true` and `false` is possibly messing with your head a little bit by now. You're probably wondering how all your `if` statements and `for` loops have been working, if they've included compound logical expressions like `a && (b || c)`.

Don't worry! The sky is not falling. Your code is (probably) just fine. It's just that you probably never realized before that there was an *implicit* coercion to `boolean` going on *after* the compound expression was evaluated.

Consider:

```
var a = 42;
var b = null;
var c = "foo";

if (a && (b || c)) {
    console.log( "yep" );
}
```

This code still works the way you always thought it did, except for one subtle extra detail. The `a && (b || c)` expression *actually* results in `"foo"`, not `true`. So, the `if` statement *then* forces the `"foo"` value to coerce to a `boolean`, which of course will be `true`.

See? No reason to panic. Your code is probably still safe. But now you know more about how it does what it does.

And now you also realize that such code is using *implicit* coercion. If you're in the "avoid (implicit) coercion camp" still, you're going to need to go back and make all of those tests *explicit*:

```
if (!!a && (!!b || !!c)) {
    console.log( "yep" );
}
```

Good luck with that! ... Sorry, just teasing.

Symbol Coercion

Up to this point, there's been almost no observable outcome difference between *explicit* and *implicit* coercion—only the readability of code has been at stake.

But ES6 Symbols introduce a gotcha into the coercion system that we need to discuss briefly. For reasons that go well beyond the scope of what we'll discuss in this book, *explicit* coercion of a `symbol` to a string is allowed, but *implicit* coercion of the same is disallowed and throws an error.

Consider:

```
var s1 = Symbol( "cool" );
String( s1 );      // "Symbol(cool)"

var s2 = Symbol( "not cool" );
s2 + "";           // TypeError
```

symbol values cannot coerce to number at all (throws an error either way), but strangely they can both *explicitly* and *implicitly* coerce to boolean (always true).

Consistency is always easier to learn, and exceptions are never fun to deal with, but we just need to be careful around the new ES6 symbol values and how we coerce them.

The good news: it's probably going to be exceedingly rare for you to need to coerce a symbol value. The way they're typically used (see Chapter 3) will probably not call for coercion on a normal basis.

Loose Equals Versus Strict Equals

Loose equals is the == operator, and strict equals is the === operator. Both operators are used for comparing two values for "equality," but the "loose" versus "strict" indicates a very important difference in behavior between the two, specifically in how they decide "equality."

A very common misconception about these two operators is: "== checks values for equality and === checks both values and types for equality." While that sounds nice and reasonable, it's inaccurate. Countless well-respected JavaScript books and blogs have said exactly that, but unfortunately they're all *wrong*.

The correct description is: "== allows coercion in the equality comparison and === disallows coercion."

Equality Performance

Stop and think about the difference between the first (inaccurate) explanation and this second (accurate) one.

In the first explanation, it seems obvious that === is *doing more work* than ==, because it has to *also* check the type. In the second explanation, == is the one *doing more work* because it has to follow through the steps of coercion if the types are different.

Don't fall into the trap, as many have, of thinking this has anything to do with performance, though, as if == is going to be slower than === in any relevant way. While it's measurable that coercion does take *a little bit* of processing time, it's mere microseconds (yes, that's millionths of a second!).

If you're comparing two values of the same types, == and === use the identical algorithm, and so other than minor differences in engine implementation, they should do the same work.

If you're comparing two values of different types, the performance isn't the important factor. What you should be asking yourself is, when comparing these two values, do I want coercion or not?

If you want coercion, use == loose equality, but if you don't want coercion, use === strict equality.

 The implication here then is that both == and === check the types of their operands. The difference is in how they respond if the types don't match.

Abstract Equality

The == operator's behavior is defined as "The Abstract Equality Comparison Algorithm" in section 11.9.3 of the ES5 spec. What's listed there is a comprehensive but simple algorithm that explicitly states every possible combination of types, and how the coercions (if necessary) should happen for each combination.

When (*implicit*) coercion is maligned as being too complicated and too flawed to be a *useful good part*, it is these rules of "abstract equality" that are being condemned. Generally, they are said to be too complex and too unintuitive for developers to practically learn and use, and that they are prone more to causing bugs in JS programs than to enabling greater code readability. I believe this is a flawed premise—that you readers are competent developers who write (and read and understand!) algorithms (aka code) all day long. So, what follows is a plain exposition of the "abstract equality" in simple terms. But I implore you to also read section 11.9.3 of the ES5 spec. I think you'll be surprised at just how reasonable it is.

Basically, the first clause (11.9.3.1) says that if the two values being compared are of the same type, they are simply and naturally compared via Identity as you'd expect. For example, 42 is only equal to 42, and "abc" is only equal to "abc".

Some minor exceptions to normal expectation to be aware of:

- NaN is never equal to itself (see Chapter 2).
- +0 and -0 are equal to each other (see Chapter 2).

The final provision in clause 11.9.3.1 is for == loose equality comparison with objects (including functions and arrays). Two such values are only *equal* if they are both references to *the exact same value*. No coercion occurs here.

The === strict equality comparison is defined identically to 11.9.3.1, including the provision about two object values. It's a very little known fact that == and === behave identically in the case where two objects are being compared!

The rest of the algorithm in 11.9.3 specifies that if you use == loose equality to compare two values of different types, one or both of the values will need to be *implicitly* coerced. This coercion happens so that both values eventually end up as the same type, which can then directly be compared for equality using simple value Identity.

The != loose not-equality operation is defined exactly as you'd expect, in that it's literally the == operation comparison performed in its entirety, then the negation of the result. The same goes for the !== strict not-equality operation.

Comparing: strings to numbers

To illustrate == coercion, let's first build off the string and number examples earlier in this chapter:

```
var a = 42;
var b = "42";

a === b;    // false
a == b;     // true
```

As we'd expect, a === b fails, because no coercion is allowed, and indeed the 42 and "42" values are different.

However, the second comparison a == b uses loose equality, which means that if the types happen to be different, the comparison algorithm will perform *implicit* coercion on one or both values.

But exactly what kind of coercion happens here? Does the a value of 42 become a string, or does the b value of "42" become a number?

In the ES5 spec, clauses 11.9.3.4-5 say:

1. If Type(x) is Number and Type(y) is String, return the result of the comparison x == ToNumber(y).

2. If Type(x) is String and Type(y) is Number, return the result of the comparison ToNumber(x) == y.

The spec uses Number and String as the formal names for the types, while this book prefers number and string for the primitive types. Do not let the capitalization of Number in the spec confuse you for the Number() native function. For our purposes, the capitalization of the type name is irrelevant—they have basically the same meaning.

Clearly, the spec says the "42" value is coerced to a number for the comparison. The *how* of that coercion has already been covered earlier, specifically with the ToNumber abstract operation. In this case, it's quite obvious then that the resulting two 42 values are equal.

Comparing: anything to boolean

One of the biggest gotchas with the *implicit* coercion of == loose equality pops up when you try to compare a value directly to true or false.

Consider:

```
var a = "42";
var b = true;

a == b; // false
```

Wait, what happened here!? We know that "42" is a truthy value (see earlier in this chapter). So, how come it's not == loose equal to true?

The reason is both simple and deceptively tricky. It's so easy to mis-understand, many JS developers never pay close enough attention to fully grasp it.

Let's again quote the spec, clauses 11.9.3.6-7:

1. If Type(x) is Boolean, return the result of the comparison ToNumber(x) == y.

2. If Type(y) is Boolean, return the result of the comparison x == ToNumber(y).

Let's break that down. First:

```
var x = true;
var y = "42";

x == y; // false
```

The Type(x) is indeed Boolean, so it performs ToNumber(x), which coerces true to 1. Now, 1 == "42" is evaluated. The types are still different, so (essentially recursively) we reconsult the algorithm, which just as above will coerce "42" to 42, and 1 == 42 is clearly false.

Reverse it, and we still get the same outcome:

```
var x = "42";
var y = false;

x == y; // false
```

The Type(y) is Boolean this time, so ToNumber(y) yields 0. "42" ==
0 recursively becomes 42 == 0, which is of course false.

In other words, the value "42" is neither == true nor == false. At
first, that statement might seem crazy. How can a value be neither
truthy nor falsy?

But that's the problem! You're asking the wrong question, entirely.
It's not your fault, really. Your brain is tricking you.

"42" is indeed truthy, but "42" == true is not performing a
boolean test/coercion at all, no matter what your brain says. "42" *is
not* being coerced to a boolean (true), but instead true is being
coerced to a 1, and then "42" is being coerced to 42.

Whether we like it or not, ToBoolean is not even involved here, so
the truthiness or falsiness of "42" is irrelevant to the == operation!

What *is* relevant is to understand how the == comparison algorithm
behaves with all the different type combinations. As it regards a
boolean value on either side of the ==, a boolean always coerces to a
number *first*.

If that seems strange to you, you're not alone. I personally would
recommend to never, ever, under any circumstances, use == true or
== false. Ever.

But remember, I'm only talking about == here. === true and ===
false wouldn't allow the coercion, so they're safe from this hidden
ToNumber coercion.

Consider:

```
var a = "42";

// bad (will fail!):
if (a == true) {
    // ..
}

// also bad (will fail!):
if (a === true) {
    // ..
}

// good enough (works implicitly):
if (a) {
    // ..
```

```
}

// better (works explicitly):
if (!!a) {
    // ..
}

// also great (works explicitly):
if (Boolean( a )) {
    // ..
}
```

If you avoid ever using == true or == false (aka loose equality
with booleans) in your code, you'll never have to worry about this
truthiness/falsiness mental gotcha.

Comparing: nulls to undefineds

Another example of *implicit* coercion can be seen with == loose
equality between null and undefined values. Yet again quoting the
ES5 spec, clauses 11.9.3.2-3:

1. If x is null and y is undefined, return true.

2. If x is undefined and y is null, return true.

null and undefined, when compared with == loose equality, equate
to (aka coerce to) each other (as well as themselves, obviously), and
no other values in the entire language.

What this means is that null and undefined can be treated as indistinguishable for comparison purposes, if you use the == loose equality operator to allow their mutual *implicit* coercion:

```
var a = null;
var b;

a == b;     // true
a == null;  // true
b == null;  // true

a == false; // false
b == false; // false
a == "";    // false
b == "";    // false
a == 0;     // false
b == 0;     // false
```

The coercion between null and undefined is safe and predictable, and no other values can give false positives in such a check. I recommend using this coercion to allow null and undefined to be indistinguishable and thus treated as the same value.

For example:

```
var a = doSomething();

if (a == null) {
    // ..
}
```

The a == null check will pass only if doSomething() returns either null or undefined, and will fail with any other value, even other falsy values like 0, false, and "".

The *explicit* form of the check, which disallows any such coercion, is (I think) unnecessarily much uglier (and perhaps a tiny bit less performant!):

```
var a = doSomething();

if (a === undefined || a === null) {
    // ..
}
```

In my opinion, the form a == null is yet another example where *implicit* coercion improves code readability, but does so in a reliably safe way.

Comparing: objects to nonobjects

If an object/function/array is compared to a simple scalar primitive (string, number, or boolean), the ES5 spec says in clauses 11.9.3.8-9:

1. If Type(x) is either String or Number and Type(y) is Object, return the result of the comparison x == ToPrimitive(y).

2. If Type(x) is Object and Type(y) is either String or Number, return the result of the comparison ToPrimitive(x) == y.

You may notice that these clauses only mention String and Number, but not Boolean. That's because, as quoted earlier, clauses 11.9.3.6-7 take care of coercing any Boolean operand presented to a Number first.

Consider:

```
var a = 42;
var b = [ 42 ];

a == b; // true
```

The [42] value has its ToPrimitive abstract operation called (see "Abstract Value Operations" on page 59), which results in the "42" value. From there, it's just "42" == 42, which as we've already covered becomes 42 == 42, so a and b are found to be coercively equal.

All the quirks of the ToPrimitive abstract operation that we discussed earlier in this chapter (toString(), valueOf()) apply here as you'd expect. This can be quite useful if you have a complex data structure that you want to define a custom valueOf() method on, to provide a simple value for equality comparison purposes.

In Chapter 3, we covered "unboxing," where an object wrapper around a primitive value (like from new String("abc"), for instance) is unwrapped, and the underlying primitive value ("abc") is returned. This behavior is related to the ToPrimitive coercion in the == algorithm:

```
var a = "abc";
var b = Object( a );    // same as `new String( a )`

a === b;                // false
a == b;                 // true
```

a == b is true because b is coerced (aka "unboxed," unwrapped) via ToPrimitive to its underlying "abc" simple scalar primitive value, which is the same as the value in a.

There are some values where this is not the case, though, because of other overriding rules in the == algorithm. Consider:

```
var a = null;
var b = Object( a );    // same as `Object()`
a == b;                 // false

var c = undefined;
var d = Object( c );    // same as `Object()`
c == d;                 // false

var e = NaN;
var f = Object( e );    // same as `new Number( e )`
e == f;                 // false
```

The null and undefined values cannot be boxed—they have no object wrapper equivalent—so Object(null) is just like Object() in that both just produce a normal object.

NaN can be boxed to its Number object wrapper equivalent, but when == causes an unboxing, the NaN == NaN comparison fails because NaN is never equal to itself (see Chapter 2).

Edge Cases

Now that we've thoroughly examined how the *implicit* coercion of == loose equality works (in both sensible and surprising ways), let's try to call out the worst, craziest corner cases so we can see what we need to avoid to not get bitten with coercion bugs.

First, let's examine how modifying the built-in native prototypes can produce crazy results:

A number by any other value would...

```
Number.prototype.valueOf = function() {
    return 3;
};

new Number( 2 ) == 3;    // true
```

 2 == 3 would not have fallen into this trap, because neither 2 nor 3 would have invoked the built-in Number.prototype.valueOf() method because both are already primitive number values and can be compared directly. However, new Number(2) must go through the ToPrimitive coercion, and thus invoke valueOf().

Evil, huh? Of course it is. No one should ever do such a thing. The fact that you *can* do this is sometimes used as a criticism of coercion and ==. But that's misdirected frustration. JavaScript is not bad because you can do such things, a *developer* is bad if they do such things. Don't fall into the "my programming language should protect me from myself" fallacy.

Next, let's consider another tricky example, which takes the evil from the previous example to another level:

```
if (a == 2 && a == 3) {
    // ..
}
```

You might think this would be impossible, because a could never be equal to both 2 and 3 *at the same time*. But "at the same time" is inaccurate, since the first expression a == 2 happens strictly *before* a == 3.

So, what if we make a.valueOf() have side effects each time it's called, such that the first time it returns 2 and the second time it's called it returns 3? Pretty easy:

```
var i = 2;

Number.prototype.valueOf = function() {
    return i++;
};

var a = new Number( 42 );

if (a == 2 && a == 3) {
    console.log( "Yep, this happened." );
}
```

Again, these are evil tricks. Don't do them. But also don't use them as complaints against coercion. Potential abuses of a mechanism are not sufficient evidence to condemn the mechanism. Just avoid these crazy tricks, and stick only with valid and proper usage of coercion.

Falsy comparisons

The most common complaint against *implicit* coercion in == comparisons comes from how falsy values behave surprisingly when compared to each other.

To illustrate, let's look at a list of the corner cases around falsy value comparisons, to see which ones are reasonable and which are troublesome:

```
"0" == null;          // false
"0" == undefined;     // false
"0" == false;         // true -- UH OH!
"0" == NaN;           // false
"0" == 0;             // true
"0" == "";            // false

false == null;        // false
false == undefined;   // false
false == NaN;         // false
false == 0;           // true -- UH OH!
false == "";          // true -- UH OH!
false == [];          // true -- UH OH!
false == {};          // false

"" == null;           // false
"" == undefined;      // false
"" == NaN;            // false
"" == 0;              // true -- UH OH!
"" == [];             // true -- UH OH!
"" == {};             // false

0 == null;            // false
0 == undefined;       // false
0 == NaN;             // false
0 == [];              // true -- UH OH!
0 == {};              // false
```

In this list of 24 comparisons, 17 of them are quite reasonable and predictable. For example, we know that "" and NaN are not at all equatable values, and indeed they don't coerce to be loose equals, whereas "0" and 0 are reasonably equitable and *do* coerce as loose equals.

However, seven of the comparisons are marked with "UH OH!" because as false positives, they are much more likely gotchas that could trip you up. "" and 0 are definitely distinctly different values, and it's rare you'd want to treat them as equitable, so their mutual coercion is troublesome. Note that there aren't any false negatives here.

The crazy ones

We don't have to stop there, though. We can keep looking for even more troublesome coercions:

```
[] == ![];      // true
```

Oooo, that seems at a higher level of crazy, right!? Your brain may likely trick you that you're comparing a truthy to a falsy value, so the true result is surprising, as we *know* a value can never be truthy and falsy at the same time!

But that's not what's actually happening. Let's break it down. What do we know about the ! unary operator? It explicitly coerces to a boolean using the ToBoolean rules (and it also flips the parity). So before [] == ![] is even processed, it's actually already translated to [] == false. We already saw that form in our above list (false == []), so its surprise result is *not new* to us.

How about other corner cases?

```
2 == [2];       // true
"" == [null];   // true
```

As we said earlier in our ToNumber discussion, the righthand side [2] and [null] values will go through a ToPrimitive coercion so they can be more readily compared to the simple primitives (2 and "", respectively) on the lefthand side. Since the valueOf() for array values just returns the array itself, coercion falls to stringifying the array.

[2] will become "2", which then is ToNumber coerced to 2 for the righthand side value in the first comparison. [null] just straight becomes "".

So, 2 == 2 and "" == "" are completely understandable.

If your instinct is to still dislike these results, your frustration is not actually with coercion like you probably think it is. It's actually a complaint against the default array values' ToPrimitive behavior of coercing to a string value. More likely, you'd just wish that [2].toString() didn't return "2", or that [null].toString() didn't return "".

But what exactly *should* these string coercions result in? I can't really think of any other appropriate string coercion of [2] than

"2", except perhaps "[2]"—but that could be very strange in other contexts!

You could rightly make the case that since `String(null)` becomes "null", then `String([null])` should also become "null". That's a reasonable assertion. So, that's the real culprit.

Implicit coercion itself isn't the evil here. Even an *explicit coercion* of `[null]` to a string results in "". What's at odds is whether it's sensible at all for `array` values to stringify to the equivalent of their contents, and exactly how that happens. So, direct your frustration at the rules for `String( [..] )`, because that's where the craziness stems from. Perhaps there should be no stringification coercion of `array`s at all? But that would have lots of other downsides in other parts of the language.

Another famously cited gotcha:

```
0 == "\n";      // true
```

As we discussed earlier with empty "", "\n" (or " " or any other whitespace combination) is coerced via `ToNumber`, and the result is 0. What other `number` value would you expect whitespace to coerce to? Does it bother you that *explicit* `Number(" ")` yields 0?

Really the only other reasonable `number` value that empty strings or whitespace strings could coerce to is `NaN`. But would that *really* be better? The comparison " " == `NaN` would of course fail, but it's unclear that we'd have really *fixed* any of the underlying concerns.

The chances that a real-world JS program fails because 0 == "\n" are awfully rare, and such corner cases are easy to avoid.

Type conversions *always* have corner cases, in any language—nothing specific to coercion. The issues here are about second-guessing a certain set of corner cases (and perhaps rightly so!?), but that's not a salient argument against the overall coercion mechanism.

Bottom line: almost any crazy coercion between *normal values* that you're likely to run into (aside from intentionally tricky `valueOf()` or `toString()` hacks as earlier) will boil down to the short seven-item list of gotcha coercions we've identified above.

To contrast against these 24 likely suspects for coercion gotchas, consider another list like this:

```
42 == "43";                    // false
"foo" == 42;                   // false
"true" == true;                // false

42 == "42";                    // true
"foo" == [ "foo" ];            // true
```

In these nonfalsy, noncorner cases (and there are literally an infinite number of comparisons we could put on this list), the coercion results are totally safe, reasonable, and explainable.

Sanity check

OK, we've definitely found some crazy stuff when we've looked deeply into *implicit* coercion. No wonder that most developers claim coercion is evil and should be avoided, right!?

But let's take a step back and do a sanity check.

By way of magnitude comparison, we have *a list* of seven troublesome gotcha coercions, but we have *another list* of (at least 17, but actually infinite) coercions that are totally sane and explainable.

If you're looking for a textbook example of "throwing the baby out with the bathwater," this is it: discarding the entirety of coercion (the infinitely large list of safe and useful behaviors) because of a list of literally just seven gotchas.

The more prudent reaction would be to ask, "How can I use the countless *good parts* of coercion, but avoid the few *bad parts*?"

Let's look again at the *bad* list:

```
"0" == false;                  // true -- UH OH!
false == 0;                    // true -- UH OH!
false == "";                   // true -- UH OH!
false == [];                   // true -- UH OH!
"" == 0;                       // true -- UH OH!
"" == [];                      // true -- UH OH!
0 == [];                       // true -- UH OH!
```

Four of the seven items on this list involve == false comparison, which we said earlier you should always, always avoid. That's a pretty easy rule to remember.

Now the list is down to three.

```
"" == 0;                       // true -- UH OH!
"" == [];                      // true -- UH OH!
0 == [];                       // true -- UH OH!
```

Are these reasonable coercions you'd do in a normal JavaScript program? Under what conditions would they really happen?

I don't think it's terribly likely that you'd literally use `==` `[]` in a `boolean` test in your program, at least not if you know what you're doing. You'd probably instead be doing `== ""` or `== 0`, like:

```
function doSomething(a) {
    if (a == "") {
        // ..
    }
}
```

You'd have an oops if you accidentally called `doSomething(0)` or `doS omething([])`. Another scenario:

```
function doSomething(a,b) {
    if (a == b) {
        // ..
    }
}
```

Again, this could break if you did something like `doSomething("", 0)` or `doSomething([],"")`.

So, while the situations *can* exist where these coercions will bite you, and you'll want to be careful around them, they're probably not super common on the whole of your code base.

Safely using implicit coercion

The most important advice I can give you: examine your program and reason about what values can show up on either side of an `==` comparison. To effectively avoid issues with such comparisons, here's some heuristic rules to follow:

- If either side of the comparison can have `true` or `false` values, don't ever, EVER use `==`.
- If either side of the comparison can have `[]`, `""`, or `0` values, seriously consider not using `==`.

In these scenarios, it's almost certainly better to use `===` instead of `==`, to avoid unwanted coercion. Follow those two simple rules and pretty much all the coercion gotchas that could reasonably hurt you will effectively be avoided.

Being more explicit/verbose in these cases will save you from a lot of headaches.

The question of == versus === is really appropriately framed as: should you allow coercion for a comparison or not?

There's lots of cases where such coercion can be helpful, allowing you to more tersely express some comparison logic (like with null and undefined, for example).

In the overall scheme of things, there's relatively few cases where *implicit* coercion is truly dangerous. But in those places, for safety sake, definitely use ===.

 Another place where coercion is guaranteed *not* to bite you is with the typeof operator. typeof is always going to return you one of seven strings (see Chapter 1), and none of them are the empty "" string. As such, there's no case where checking the type of some value is going to run afoul of *implicit* coercion. typeof x == "function" is 100% as safe and reliable as typeof x === "function". Literally, the spec says the algorithm will be identical in this situation. So, don't just blindly use === everywhere simply because that's what your code tools tell you to do, or (worst of all) because you've been told in some book to not think about it. You own the quality of your code.

Is *implicit* coercion evil and dangerous? In a few cases, yes, but overwhelmingly, no.

Be a responsible and mature developer. Learn how to use the power of coercion (both *explicit* and *implicit*) effectively and safely. And teach those around you to do the same.

Figure 4-1 shows a handy table made by GitHub user Alex Dorey (@dorey on GitHub) to visualize a variety of comparisons.

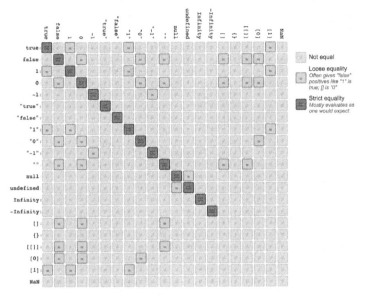

Figure 4-1. Equality in JavaScript (https://github.com/dorey/JavaScript-Equality-Table)

Abstract Relational Comparison

While this part of *implicit* coercion often gets a lot less attention, it's important nonetheless to think about what happens with a < b comparisons (similar to how we just examined a == b in depth).

The "Abstract Relational Comparison" algorithm in ES5 section 11.8.5 essentially divides itself into two parts: what to do if the comparison involves both string values (second half), or anything else (first half).

 The algorithm is only defined for a < b. So, a > b is handled as b < a.

The algorithm first calls ToPrimitive coercion on both values, and if the return result of either call is not a string, then both values are coerced to number values using the ToNumber operation rules, and compared numerically.

For example:

```
var a = [ 42 ];
var b = [ "43" ];

a < b;  // true
b < a;  // false
```

 Similar caveats for -0 and NaN apply here as they did in the == algorithm discussed earlier.

However, if both values are strings for the < comparison, simple lexicographic (natural alphabetic) comparison on the characters is performed:

```
var a = [ "42" ];
var b = [ "043" ];

a < b;  // false
```

a and b are *not* coerced to numbers, because both of them end up as strings after the ToPrimitive coercion on the two arrays. So, "42" is compared character by character to "043", starting with the first characters "4" and "0", respectively. Since "0" is lexicographically *less than* "4", the comparison returns false.

The exact same behavior and reasoning goes for:

```
var a = [ 4, 2 ];
var b = [ 0, 4, 3 ];

a < b;  // false
```

Here, a becomes "4,2" and b becomes "0,4,3", and those lexicographically compare identically to the previous snippet.

What about:

```
var a = { b: 42 };
var b = { b: 43 };

a < b;  // ??
```

a < b is also false, because a becomes [object Object] and b becomes [object Object], and so clearly a is not lexicographically less than b.

But strangely:

```
var a = { b: 42 };
var b = { b: 43 };

a < b;  // false
a == b; // false
a > b;  // false

a <= b; // true
a >= b; // true
```

Why is a == b not true? They're the same string value ("[object Object]"), so it seems they should be equal, right? Nope. Recall the previous discussion about how == works with object references.

But then how are a <= b and a >= b resulting in true, if a < b *and* a == b *and* a > b are all false?

Because the spec says for a <= b, it will actually evaluate b < a first, and then negate that result. Since b < a is *also* false, the result of a <= b is true.

That's probably awfully contrary to how you might have explained what <= does up to now, which would likely have been the literal "less than *or* equal to." JS more accurately considers <= as "not greater than" (!(a > b), which JS treats as !(b < a)). Moreover, a >= b is explained by first considering it as b <= a, and then applying the same reasoning.

Unfortunately, there is no "strict relational comparison" as there is for equality. In other words, there's no way to prevent *implicit coercion* from occurring with relational comparisons like a < b, other than to ensure that a and b are of the same type explicitly before making the comparison.

Use the same reasoning from our earlier == versus === sanity check discussion. If coercion is helpful and reasonably safe, like in a 42 < "43" comparison, *use it*. On the other hand, if you need to be safe about a relational comparison, *explicitly coerce* the values first, before using < (or its counterparts):

```
var a = [ 42 ];
var b = "043";

a < b;                     // false -- string comparison!
Number( a ) < Number( b ); // true -- number comparison!
```

Review

In this chapter, we turned our attention to how JavaScript type conversions happen, called *coercion*, which can be characterized as either *explicit* or *implicit*.

Coercion gets a bad rap, but it's actually quite useful in many cases. An important task for the responsible JS developer is to take the time to learn all the ins and outs of coercion to decide which parts will help improve their code, and which parts they really should avoid.

Explicit coercion is code where it is obvious that the intent is to convert a value from one type to another. The benefit is improvement in readability and maintainability of code by reducing confusion.

Implicit coercion is coercion that is "hidden" as a side effect of some other operation, where it's not as obvious that the type conversion will occur. While it may seem that *implicit* coercion is the opposite of *explicit* and is thus bad (and indeed, many think so!), actually *implicit* coercion is also about improving the readability of code.

Especially for the *implicit* type, coercion must be used responsibly and consciously. Know why you're writing the code you're writing, and how it works. Strive to write code that others will easily be able to learn from and understand as well.

CHAPTER 5

Grammar

The last major topic we want to tackle is how JavaScript's language syntax works (aka its grammar). You may think you know how to write JS, but there's an awful lot of nuance to various parts of the language grammar that lead to confusion and misconception, so we want to dive into those parts and clear some things up.

 The term "grammar" may be a little less familiar to readers than the term "syntax." In many ways, they are similar terms, describing the *rules* for how the language works. There are nuanced differences, but they mostly don't matter for our discussion here. The grammar for JavaScript is a structured way to describe how the syntax (operators, keywords, etc.) fits together into well-formed, valid programs. In other words, discussing syntax without grammar would leave out a lot of the important details. So our focus here in this chapter is most accurately described as *grammar*, even though the raw syntax of the language is what developers directly interact with.

Statements & Expressions

It's fairly common for developers to assume that the term "statement" and "expression" are roughly equivalent. But here we need to distinguish between the two, because there are some very important differences in our JS programs.

To draw the distinction, let's borrow from terminology you may be more familiar with: the English language.

A "sentence" is one complete formation of words that expresses a thought. It's comprised of one or more "phrases," each of which can be connected with punctuation marks or conjunctions ("and," "or," etc.). A phrase can itself be made up of smaller phrases. Some phrases are incomplete and don't accomplish much by themselves, while other phrases can stand on their own. These rules are collectively called the *grammar* of the English language.

And so it goes with JavaScript grammar. Statements are sentences, expressions are phrases, and operators are conjunctions/punctuation.

Every expression in JS can be evaluated down to a single, specific value result. For example:

```
var a = 3 * 6;
var b = a;
b;
```

In this snippet, 3 * 6 is an expression (evaluates to the value 18). But a on the second line is also an expression, as is b on the third line. The a and b expressions both evaluate to the values stored in those variables at that moment, which also happens to be 18.

Moreover, each of the three lines is a statement containing expressions. var a = 3 * 6 and var b = a are called "declaration statements" because they each declare a variable (and optionally assign a value to it). The a = 3 * 6 and b = a assignments (minus the vars) are called assignment expressions.

The third line contains just the expression b, but it's also a statement all by itself (though not a terribly interesting one!). As such, this is generally referred to as an "expression statement."

Statement Completion Values

It's a fairly little known fact that statements all have completion values (even if that value is just undefined).

How would you even go about seeing the completion value of a statement?

The most obvious answer is to type the statement into your browser's developer console, because when you execute it, the console by default reports the completion value of the most recent statement it executed.

Let's consider var b = a. What's the completion value of that statement?

The b = a assignment expression results in the value that was assigned (18 above), but the var statement itself results in undefined. Why? Because var statements are defined that way in the spec. If you put var a = 42; into your console, you'll see undefined reported back instead of 42.

> Technically, it's a little more complex than that. In the ES5 spec, section 12.2 "Variable Statement," the VariableDeclaration algorithm actually *does* return a value (a string containing the name of the variable declared—weird, huh!?), but that value is basically swallowed up (except for use by the for..in loop) by the VariableStatement algorithm, which forces an empty (aka undefined) completion value.

In fact, if you've done much code experimenting in your console (or in a JavaScript environment REPL—read/evaluate/print/loop tool), you've probably seen undefined reported after many different statements, and perhaps never realized why or what that was. Put simply, the console is reporting the statement's completion value.

But what the console prints out for the completion value isn't something we can use inside our program. So how can we capture the completion value?

That's a much more complicated task. Before we explain *how*, let's explore *why* would you want to do that.

We need to consider other types of statement completion values. For example, any regular { .. } block has a completion value of the completion value of its last contained statement/expression.

Consider:

```
var b;

if (true) {
    b = 4 + 38;
}
```

If you typed that into your console/REPL, you'd probably see 42 reported, since 42 is the completion value of the if block, which took on the completion value of its last expression statement b = 4 + 38.

In other words, the completion value of a block is like an *implicit return* of the last statement value in the block.

This is conceptually familiar in languages like CoffeeScript, which have implicit return values from functions that are the same as the last statement value in the function.

But there's an obvious problem. This kind of code doesn't work:

```
var a, b;

a = if (true) {
    b = 4 + 38;
};
```

We can't capture the completion value of a statement and assign it into another variable in any easy syntactic/grammatical way (at least not yet!).

So, what can we do?

For demo purposes only—don't actually do the following in your real code!

We could use the much maligned eval(..) (sometimes pronounced "evil") function to capture this completion value:

```
var a, b;

a = eval( "if (true) { b = 4 + 38; }" );

a;  // 42
```

Yeeeaaahhhh. That's terribly ugly. But it works! And it illustrates the point that statement completion values are a real thing that can be captured not just in our console but in our programs.

There's a proposal for ES7 called the "do expression." Here's how it might work:

```
var a, b;

a = do {
    if (true) {
        b = 4 + 38;
    }
};

a;  // 42
```

The do { .. } expression executes a block (with one or many statements in it), and the final statement completion value inside the block becomes the completion value *of* the do expression, which can then be assigned to a as shown.

The general idea is to be able to treat statements as expressions—they can show up inside other statements—without needing to wrap them in an inline function expression and perform an explicit return ...

For now, statement completion values are not much more than trivia. But they're probably going to take on more significance as JS evolves, and hopefully do { .. } expressions will reduce the temptation to use stuff like eval(..).

 Repeating my earlier admonition: avoid eval(..). Seriously. See the *Scope & Closures* title in this series for more explanation.

Expression Side Effects

Most expressions don't have side effects. For example:

```
var a = 2;
var b = a + 3;
```

The expression a + 3 did not *itself* have a side effect, like for instance changing a. It had a result, which is 5, and that result was assigned to b in the statement b = a + 3.

The most common example of an expression with (possible) side effects is a function call expression:

```
function foo() {
    a = a + 1;
}

var a = 1;
foo();      // result: `undefined`, side effect: changed `a`
```

There are other side-effecting expressions, though. For example:

```
var a = 42;
var b = a++;
```

The expression a++ has two separate behaviors. *First*, it returns the current value of a, which is 42 (which then gets assigned to b). But *next*, it changes the value of a itself, incrementing it by one:

```
var a = 42;
var b = a++;

a;  // 43
b;  // 42
```

Many developers would mistakenly believe that b has value 43 just like a does. But the confusion comes from not fully considering the *when* of the side effects of the ++ operator.

The ++ increment operator and the -- decrement operator are both unary operators (see Chapter 4), which can be used in either a post-fix ("after") position or prefix ("before") position:

```
var a = 42;

a++;    // 42
a;      // 43

++a;    // 44
a;      // 44
```

When ++ is used in the prefix position as ++a, its side effect (incrementing a) happens *before* the value is returned from the expression, rather than *after* as with a++.

Would you think ++a++ was legal syntax? If you try it, you'll get a `ReferenceError` error, but why? Because side-effecting operators require a variable reference to target their side effects to. For ++a++, the a++ part is evaluated first (because of operator precedence—see below), which gives back the value of a *before* the increment. But then it tries to evaluate ++42, which (if you try it) gives the same `ReferenceError` error, since ++ can't have a side effect directly on a value like 42.

It is sometimes mistakenly thought that you can encapsulate the *after* side effect of a++ by wrapping it in a ( ) pair, like:

```
var a = 42;
var b = (a++);

a;  // 43
b;  // 42
```

Unfortunately, ( ) itself doesn't define a new wrapped expression that would be evaluated *after* the *after side effect* of the a++ expression, as we might have hoped. In fact, even if it did, a++ returns 42 first, and unless you have another expression that reevaluates a after the side effect of ++, you're not going to get 43 from that expression, so b will not be assigned 43.

There's an option, though: the , statement-series comma operator. This operator allows you to string together multiple standalone expression statements into a single statement:

```
var a = 42, b;
b = ( a++, a );

a;  // 43
b;  // 43
```

The (..) around a++, a is required here. The reason is operator precedence, which we'll cover later in this chapter.

The expression a++, a means that the second a statement expression gets evaluated *after* the *after side effects* of the a++ expression, which means it returns the 43 value for assignment to b.

Another example of a side-effecting operator is delete. As we showed in Chapter 2, delete is used to remove a property from an object or a slot from an array. But it's usually just called as a stand-alone statement:

```
var obj = {
    a: 42
};

obj.a;          // 42
delete obj.a;   // true
obj.a;          // undefined
```

The result value of the delete operator is true if the requested operation is valid/allowable, or false otherwise. But the side effect of the operator is that it removes the property (or array slot).

 What do we mean by valid/allowable? Nonexistent properties, or properties that exist and are configurable (see Chapter 3 of the *this & Object Prototypes* title in this series) will return true from the delete operator. Otherwise, the result will be false or an error.

One last example of a side-effecting operator, which may at once be both obvious and nonobvious, is the = assignment operator.

Consider:

```
var a;

a = 42;     // 42
a;          // 42
```

It may not seem like = in a = 42 is a side-effecting operator for the expression. But if we examine the result value of the a = 42 statement, it's the value that was just assigned (42), so the assignment of that same value into a is essentially a side effect.

The same reasoning about side effects goes for the compound-assignment operators like +=, -=, etc. For example, a = b += 2 is processed first as b += 2 (which is b = b + 2), and the result of *that* = assignment is then assigned to a.

This behavior that an assignment expression (or statement) results in the assigned value is primarily useful for chained assignments, such as:

```
var a, b, c;

a = b = c = 42;
```

Here, c = 42 is evaluated to 42 (with the side effect of assigning 42 to c), then b = 42 is evaluated to 42 (with the side effect of assigning 42 to b), and finally a = 42 is evaluated (with the side effect of assigning 42 to a).

 A common mistake developers make with chained assignments is like var a = b = 42. While this looks like the same thing, it's not. If that statement were to happen without there also being a separate var b (somewhere in the scope) to formally declare b, then var a = b = 42 would not declare b directly. Depending on strict mode, that would either throw an error or create an accidental global (see the *Scope & Closures* title in this series).

Another scenario to consider:

```
function vowels(str) {
    var matches;

    if (str) {
        // pull out all the vowels
        matches = str.match( /[aeiou]/g );

        if (matches) {
            return matches;
        }
    }
}

vowels( "Hello World" ); // ["e","o","o"]
```

This works, and many developers prefer such. But using an idiom where we take advantage of the assignment side effect, we can simplify by combining the two `if` statements into one:

```
function vowels(str) {
    var matches;

    // pull out all the vowels
    if (str && (matches = str.match( /[aeiou]/g ))) {
        return matches;
    }
}

vowels( "Hello World" ); // ["e","o","o"]
```

 The (..) around `matches = str.match..` is required. The reason is operator precedence, which we'll cover in "Operator Precedence" on page 137.

I prefer this shorter style, as I think it makes it clearer that the two conditionals are in fact related rather than separate. But as with most stylistic choices in JS, it's purely opinion which one is *better*.

Contextual Rules

There are quite a few places in the JavaScript grammar rules where the same syntax means different things depending on where/how it's used. This kind of thing can, in isolation, cause quite a bit of confusion.

We won't exhaustively list all such cases here, but just call out a few of the common ones.

Curly braces

There's two main places (and more coming as JS evolves!) that a pair of curly braces { .. } will show up in your code. Let's take a look at each of them.

Object literals

First, as an `object` literal:

```
// assume there's a `bar()` function defined
```

```
var a = {
    foo: bar()
};
```

How do we know this is an `object` literal? Because the { .. } pair is a value that's getting assigned to `a`.

 The a reference is called an "l-value" (aka left-hand value) since it's the target of an assignment. The { .. } pair is an "r-value" (aka right-hand value) since it's used *just* as a value (in this case as the source of an assignment).

Labels

What happens if we remove the var a = part of the above snippet?

```
// assume there's a `bar()` function defined

{
    foo: bar()
}
```

A lot of developers assume that the { .. } pair is just a standalone `object` literal that doesn't get assigned anywhere. But it's actually entirely different.

Here, { .. } is just a regular code block. It's not very idiomatic in JavaScript (much more so in other languages!) to have a standalone { .. } block like that, but it's perfectly valid JS grammar. It can be especially helpful when combined with `let` block-scoping declarations (see the *Scope & Closures* title in this series).

The { .. } code block here is functionally pretty much identical to the code block being attached to some statement, like a for/while loop, if conditional, etc.

But if it's a normal block of code, what's that bizarre looking foo: bar() syntax, and how is that legal?

It's because of a little known (and, frankly, discouraged) feature in JavaScript called "labeled statements." foo is a label for the statement bar() (that has omitted its trailing ;—see "Automatic Semicolons" on page 146 later in this chapter). But what's the point of a labeled statement?

If JavaScript had a goto statement, you'd theoretically be able to say goto foo and have execution jump to that location in code. gotos are usually considered terrible coding idioms as they make code much harder to understand (aka "spaghetti code"), so it's a *very good thing* that JavaScript doesn't have a general goto.

However, JS *does* support a limited, special form of goto: labeled jumps. Both the continue and break statements can optionally accept a specified label, in which case the program flow "jumps" kind of like a goto. Consider:

```
// `foo` labeled-loop
foo: for (var i=0; i<4; i++) {
    for (var j=0; j<4; j++) {
        // whenever the loops meet, continue outer loop
        if (j == i) {
            // jump to the next iteration of
            // the `foo` labeled-loop
            continue foo;
        }

        // skip odd multiples
        if ((j * i) % 2 == 1) {
            // normal (nonlabeled) `continue` of inner loop
            continue;
        }

        console.log( i, j );
    }
}
// 1 0
// 2 0
// 2 1
// 3 0
// 3 2
```

 continue foo does not mean "go to the *foo* labeled position to continue," but rather, "continue the loop that is labeled *foo* with its next iteration." So, it's not *really* an arbitrary goto.

As you can see, we skipped over the odd-multiple 3 1 iteration, but the labeled-loop jump also skipped iterations 1 1 and 2 2.

Perhaps a slightly more useful form of the labeled-loop jump is with break __ from inside an inner loop where you want to break out of

the outer loop. Without a labeled `break`, this same logic could sometimes be rather awkward to write:

```
// `foo` labeled-loop
foo: for (var i=0; i<4; i++) {
    for (var j=0; j<4; j++) {
        if ((i * j) >= 3) {
            console.log( "stopping!", i, j );
            break foo;
        }

        console.log( i, j );
    }
}
// 0 0
// 0 1
// 0 2
// 0 3
// 1 0
// 1 1
// 1 2
// stopping! 1 3
```

break foo does not mean "go to the *foo* labeled
position to continue," but rather, "break out of
the loop/block that is labeled *foo* and continue
after it." Not exactly a goto in the traditional
sense, huh?

The nonlabeled `break` alternative to the above would probably need
to involve one or more functions, shared scope variable access, etc.
It would quite likely be more confusing than labeled `break`, so here
using a labeled `break` is perhaps the better option.

A label can apply to a nonloop block, but only `break` can reference
such a nonloop label. You can do a labeled `break` ___ out of any
labeled block, but you cannot `continue` ___ a nonloop label, nor
can you do a nonlabeled `break` out of a block:

```
// `bar` labeled-block
function foo() {
    bar: {
        console.log( "Hello" );
        break bar;
        console.log( "never runs" );
    }
    console.log( "World" );
}
```

```
foo();
// Hello
// World
```

Labeled loops/blocks are extremely uncommon, and often frowned upon. It's best to avoid them if possible; for example, by using function calls instead of the loop jumps. But there are perhaps some limited cases where they might be useful. If you're going to use a labeled jump, make sure to document what you're doing with plenty of comments!

It's a very common belief that JSON is a proper subset of JS, so a string of JSON (like {"a":42}—notice the quotes around the property name as JSON requires!) is thought to be a valid JavaScript program. Not true! Try putting {"a":42} into your JS console, and you'll get an error.

That's because statement labels cannot have quotes around them, so "a" is not a valid label, and thus : can't come right after it.

So, JSON is truly a subset of JS syntax, but JSON is not valid JS grammar by itself.

One extremely common misconception along these lines is that if you were to load a JS file into a <script src=..> tag that only has JSON content in it (like from an API call), the data would be read as valid JavaScript but just be inaccessible to the program. JSON-P (the practice of wrapping the JSON data in a function call, like foo({"a":42})) is usually said to solve this inaccessibility by sending the value to one of your program's functions.

Not true! The totally valid JSON value {"a":42} by itself would actually throw a JS error because it'd be interpreted as a statement block with an invalid label. But foo({"a":42}) is valid JS because in it, {"a":42} is an object literal value being passed to foo(..). So, properly said, *JSON-P makes JSON into valid JS grammar!*

Blocks

Another commonly cited JS gotcha (related to coercion—see Chapter 4) is:

```
[] + {}; // "[object Object]"
{} + []; // 0
```

This seems to imply the + operator gives different results depending on whether the first operand is the [] or the {}. But that actually has nothing to do with it!

On the first line, {} appears in the + operator's expression, and is therefore interpreted as an actual value (an empty object). Chapter 4 explained that [] is coerced to "" and thus {} is coerced to a string value as well: "[object Object]".

But on the second line, {} is interpreted as a standalone {} empty block (which does nothing). Blocks don't need semicolons to terminate them, so the lack of one here isn't a problem. Finally, + [] is an expression that *explicitly coerces* (see Chapter 4) the [] to a number, which is the 0 value.

Object destructuring

Starting with ES6, another place that you'll see { .. } pairs showing up is with "destructuring assignments" (see the *ES6 & Beyond* title in this series for more info), specifically object destructuring. Consider:

```
function getData() {
    // ..
    return {
        a: 42,
        b: "foo"
    };
}

var { a, b } = getData();

console.log( a, b ); // 42 "foo"
```

As you can probably tell, var { a , b } = .. is a form of ES6 destructuring assignment, which is rougly equivalent to:

```
var res = getData();
var a = res.a;
var b = res.b;
```

{ a, b } is actually ES6 destructuring shorthand for { a: a, b: b }, so either will work, but it's expected that the shorter { a, b } will be become the preferred form.

Object destructuring with a { .. } pair can also be used for named function arguments, which is sugar for this same sort of implicit object property assignment:

```
function foo({ a, b, c }) {
    // no need for:
    // var a = obj.a, b = obj.b, c = obj.c
    console.log( a, b, c );
}

foo( {
    c: [1,2,3],
    a: 42,
    b: "foo"
} );    // 42 "foo" [1, 2, 3]
```

So, the context we use { .. } pairs in entirely determines what they mean, which illustrates the difference between syntax and grammar. It's very important to understand these nuances to avoid unexpected interpretations by the JS engine.

else if and optional blocks

It's a common misconception that JavaScript has an else if clause, because you can do:

```
if (a) {
    // ..
}
else if (b) {
    // ..
}
else {
    // ..
}
```

But there's a hidden characteristic of the JS grammar here: there is no else if. But if and else statements are allowed to omit the { } around their attached block if they only contain a single statement. You've seen this many times before, undoubtedly:

```
if (a) doSomething( a );
```

Many JS style guides will insist that you always use { } around a single statement block, like:

```
if (a) { doSomething( a ); }
```

However, the exact same grammar rule applies to the else clause, so the else if form you've likely always coded is *actually* parsed as:

```
if (a) {
    // ..
}
else {
    if (b) {
        // ..
    }
    else {
        // ..
    }
}
```

The `if (b) { .. } else { .. }` is a single statement that follows the `else`, so you can either put the surrounding `{ }` in or not. In other words, when you use `else if`, you're technically breaking that common style guide rule and just defining your `else` with a single `if` statement.

Of course, the `else if` idiom is extremely common and results in one less level of indentation, so it's attractive. Whichever way you do it, just call out explicitly in your own style guide/rules and don't assume things like `else if` are direct grammar rules.

Operator Precedence

As we covered in Chapter 4, JavaScript's version of `&&` and `||` are interesting in that they select and return one of their operands, rather than just resulting in `true` or `false`. That's easy to reason about if there are only two operands and one operator:

```
var a = 42;
var b = "foo";

a && b; // "foo"
a || b; // 42
```

But what about when there's two operators involved, and three operands?

```
var a = 42;
var b = "foo";
var c = [1,2,3];

a && b || c; // ???
a || b && c; // ???
```

To understand what those expressions result in, we're going to need to understand what rules govern how the operators are processed when there's more than one present in an expression.

These rules are called "operator precedence."

I bet most readers feel they have a decent grasp on operator precedence. But as with everything else we've covered in this series, we're going to poke and prod at that understanding to see just how solid it really is, and hopefully learn a few new things along the way.

Recall the example from above:

```
var a = 42, b;
b = ( a++, a );

a;  // 43
b;  // 43
```

But what would happen if we remove the ( )?

```
var a = 42, b;
b = a++, a;

a;  // 43
b;  // 42
```

Wait! Why did that change the value assigned to b?

Because the , operator has a lower precedence than the = operator. So, b = a++, a is interpreted as (b = a++), a. Because (as we explained earlier) a++ has *after side effects*, the assigned value to b is the value 42 before the ++ changes a.

This is just a simple matter of needing to understand operator precedence. If you're going to use , as a statement-series operator, it's important to know that it actually has the lowest precedence. Every other operator will more tightly bind than , will.

Now, recall this example from above:

```
if (str && (matches = str.match( /[aeiou]/g ))) {
    // ..
}
```

We said the ( ) around the assignment is required, but why? Because && has higher precedence than =, so without the ( ) to force the binding, the expression would instead be treated as (str && matches) = str.match... But this would be an error, because the result of (`str && matches`) isn't going to be a variable, but instead a value (in this case `undefined`), and so it can't be the lefthand side of an = assignment!

OK, so you probably think you've got this operator precedence thing down.

Let's move on to a more complex example (which we'll carry throughout the next several sections of this chapter) to *really* test your understanding:

```
var a = 42;
var b = "foo";
var c = false;

var d = a && b || c ? c || b ? a : c && b : a;

d;      // ??
```

OK, evil, I admit it. No one would write a string of expressions like that, right? *Probably* not, but we're going to use it to examine various issues around chaining multiple operators together, which *is* a very common task.

The result above is 42. But that's not nearly as interesting as how we can figure out that answer without just plugging it into a JS program to let JavaScript sort it out.

Let's dig in.

The first question—it may not have even occurred to you to ask—is, does the first part (`a && b || c`) behave like (`a && b`) `|| c` or like `a && (b || c)`? Do you know for certain? Can you even convince yourself they are actually different?

```
(false && true) || true;    // true
false && (true || true);    // false
```

So, there's proof they're different. But still, how does `false && true || true` behave? The answer:

```
false && true || true;      // true
(false && true) || true;    // true
```

So we have our answer. The && operator is evaluated first and the || operator is evaluated second.

But is that just because of left-to-right processing? Let's reverse the order of operators:

```
true || false && false;      // true

(true || false) && false;    // false--nope
true || (false && false);    // true--winner, winner!
```

Now we've proved that && is evaluated first and then ||, and in this case that was actually counter to generally expected left-to-right processing.

So what caused the behavior? *Operator precedence.*

Every language defines its own operator precedence list. It's dismaying, though, just how uncommon it is that JS developers have read JS's list.

If you knew it well, the above examples wouldn't have tripped you up in the slightest, because you'd already know that && is more precedent than ||. But I bet a fair amount of readers had to think about it a little bit.

 Unfortunately, the JS spec doesn't really have its operator precedence list in a convenient, single location. You have to parse through and understand all the grammar rules. So we'll try to lay out the more common and useful bits here in a more convenient format. For a complete list of operator precedence, see "Operator Precedence" on the MDN site (*https://developer.mozilla.org/ en-US/docs/Web/JavaScript/Reference/Operators/ Operator_Precedence*).

Short Circuited

In Chapter 4, we mentioned the "short circuiting" nature of operators like && and || in a sidenote. Let's revisit that in more detail now.

For both && and || operators, the righthand operand will not be evaluated if the lefthand operand is sufficient to determine the outcome of the operation. Hence, the name "short circuited" (in that if possible, it will take an early shortcut out).

For example, with a && b, b is not evaluated if a is falsy, because the result of the && operand is already certain, so there's no point in bothering to check b. Likewise, with a || b, if a is truthy, the result of the operand is already certain, so there's no reason to check b.

This short circuiting can be very helpful and is commonly used:

```
function doSomething(opts) {
    if (opts && opts.cool) {
        // ..
    }
}
```

The opts part of the opts && opts.cool test acts as sort of a guard, because if opts is unset (or is otherwise not an object), the expression opts.cool would throw an error. The opts test failing plus the short circuiting means that opts.cool won't even be evaluated, thus no error!

Similarly, you can use || short circuiting:

```
function doSomething(opts) {
    if (opts.cache || primeCache()) {
        // ..
    }
}
```

Here, we're checking for opts.cache first, and if it's present, we don't call the primeCache() function, thus avoiding potentially unnecessary work.

Tighter Binding

But let's turn our attention back to that earlier complex statement example with all the chained operators, specifically the ? : ternary operator parts. Does the ? : operator have more or less precedence than the && and || operators?

```
a && b || c ? c || b ? a : c && b : a
```

Is that more like this?

```
a && b || (c ? c || (b ? a : c) && b : a)
```

Or more like this?

```
(a && b || c) ? (c || b) ? a : (c && b) : a
```

The answer is the second one. But why?

Because && is more precedent than ||, and || is more precedent than ? :.

So, the expression (a && b || c) is evaluated *first* before the ? : it participates in. Another way this is commonly explained is that &&

and || "bind more tightly" than ? :. If the reverse was true, then c ? c... would bind more tightly, and it would behave (as the first choice) like a && b || (c ? c..).

Associativity

So, the && and || operators bind first, then the ? : operator. But what about multiple operators of the same precedence? Do they always process left-to-right or right-to-left?

In general, operators are either left-associative or right-associative, referring to whether grouping happens from the left or from the right.

It's important to note that associativity is *not* the same thing as left-to-right or right-to-left processing.

But why does it matter whether processing is left-to-right or right-to-left? Because expressions can have side effects, like for instance with function calls:

```
var a = foo() && bar();
```

Here, foo() is evaluated first, and then possibly bar() depending on the result of the foo() expression. That definitely could result in different program behavior than if bar() was called before foo().

But this behavior is *just* left-to-right processing (the default behavior in JavaScript!)—it has nothing to do with the associativity of &&. In that example, since there's only one && and thus no relevant grouping here, associativity doesn't even come into play.

But with an expression like a && b && c, grouping *will* happen implicitly, meaning that either a && b or b && c will be evaluated first.

Technically, a && b && c will be handled as (a && b) && c, because && is left-associative (so is ||, by the way). However, the right-associative alternative a && (b && c) behaves observably the same way. For the same values, the same expressions are evaluated in the same order.

If hypothetically && was right-associative, it would be processed the same as if you manually used ( ) to create a grouping like a && (b && c). But that still doesn't mean that c would be processed before b. Right-associativity does *not* mean right-to-left evaluation, it means right-to-left *grouping*. Either way, regardless of the grouping/associativity, the strict ordering of evaluation will be a, then b, then c (aka left-to-right).

So it doesn't really matter that much that && and || are left-associative, other than to be accurate in how we discuss their definitions.

But that's not always the case. Some operators would behave very differently depending on left-associativity versus right-associativity.

Consider the ? : ("ternary" or "conditional") operator:

```
a ? b : c ? d : e;
```

? : is right-associative, so which grouping represents how it will be processed?

- a ? b : (c ? d : e)
- (a ? b : c) ? d : e

The answer is a ? b : (c ? d : e). Unlike with && and || above, the right-associativity here actually matters, as (a ? b : c) ? d : e *will* behave differently for some (but not all!) combinations of values.

One such example:

```
true ? false : true ? true : true;      // false

true ? false : (true ? true : true);    // false
(true ? false : true) ? true : true;    // true
```

Even more nuanced differences lurk with other value combinations, even if the end result is the same. Consider:

```
true ? false : true ? true : false;      // false

true ? false : (true ? true : false);    // false
(true ? false : true) ? true : false;    // false
```

From that scenario, the same end result implies that the grouping is moot. However:

```
var a = true, b = false, c = true, d = true, e = false;

a ? b : (c ? d : e); // false, evaluates only `a` and `b`
(a ? b : c) ? d : e; // false, evaluates `a`, `b` AND `e`
```

So, we've clearly proved that ? : is right-associative, and that it actually matters with respect to how the operator behaves if chained with itself.

Another example of right-associativity (grouping) is the = operator. Recall the chained assignment example from earlier in the chapter:

```
var a, b, c;

a = b = c = 42;
```

We asserted earlier that a = b = c = 42 is processed by first evaluating the c = 42 assignment, then b = .., and finally a = ... Why? Because of the right-associativity, which actually treats the statement like this: a = (b = (c = 42)).

Remember our running complex assignment expression example from earlier in the chapter?

```
var a = 42;
var b = "foo";
var c = false;

var d = a && b || c ? c || b ? a : c && b : a;

d;        // 42
```

Armed with our knowledge of precedence and associativity, we should now be able to break the code down into its grouping behavior like this:

```
((a && b) || c) ? ((c || b) ? a : (c && b)) : a
```

Or, to present it indented if that's easier to understand:

```
(
  (a && b)
    ||
  c
)
  ?
(
  (c || b)
```

```
        ?
    a
        :
    (c && b)
    )
        :
    a
```

Let's solve it now:

1. (a && b) is "foo".

2. "foo" || c is "foo".

3. For the first ? test, "foo" is truthy.

4. (c || b) is "foo".

5. For the second ? test, "foo" is truthy.

6. a is 42.

That's it, we're done! The answer is 42, just as we saw earlier. That actually wasn't so hard, was it?

Disambiguation

You should now have a much better grasp on operator precedence (and associativity) and feel much more comfortable understanding how code with multiple chained operators will behave.

But an important question remains: should we all write code understanding and perfectly relying on all the rules of operator precedence/associativity? Should we only use ( ) manual grouping when it's necessary to force a different processing binding/order?

Or, on the other hand, should we recognize that even though such rules *are in fact* learnable, there's enough gotchas to warrant ignoring automatic precedence/associativity? If so, should we thus always use ( ) manual grouping and remove all reliance on these automatic behaviors?

This debate is highly subjective, and heavily symmetrical to the debate in Chapter 4 over *implicit* coercion. Most developers feel the same way about both debates: either they accept both behaviors and code expecting them, or they discard both behaviors and stick to manual/explicit idioms.

Of course, I cannot answer this question definitively for the reader here anymore than I could in Chapter 4. But I've presented you the pros and cons, and hopefully encouraged enough deeper understanding that you can make informed rather than hype-driven decisions.

In my opinion, there's an important middle ground. We should mix both operator precedence/associativity *and* ( ) manual grouping into our programs—I argue the same way in Chapter 4 for healthy/safe usage of *implicit* coercion, but certainly don't endorse it exclusively without bounds.

For example, if (a && b && c) .. is perfectly OK to me, and I wouldn't do if ((a && b) && c) .. just to explicitly call out the associativity, because I think it's overly verbose.

On the other hand, if I needed to chain two ? : conditional operators together, I'd certainly use ( ) manual grouping to make it absolutely clear what my intended logic is.

Thus, my advice here is similar to that of Chapter 4: use operator precedence/associativity where it leads to shorter and cleaner code, but use ( ) manual grouping in places where it helps create clarity and reduce confusion.

Automatic Semicolons

ASI (Automatic Semicolon Insertion) is when JavaScript assumes a ; in certain places in your JS program even if you didn't put one there.

Why would it do that? Because if you omit even a single required ; your program would fail. Not very forgiving. ASI allows JS to be tolerant of certain places where ; isn't commonly thought to be necessary.

It's important to note that ASI will only take effect in the presence of a newline (aka line break). Semicolons are not inserted in the middle of a line.

Basically, if the JS parser parses a line where a parser error would occur (a missing expected ;), and it can reasonably insert one, it does so. What's reasonable for insertion? Only if there's nothing but whitespace and/or comments between the end of some statement and that line's newline/line break.

Consider:

```
var a = 42, b
c;
```

Should JS treat the c on the next line as part of the var statement? It certainly would if a , had come anywhere (even another line) between b and c. But since there isn't one, JS assumes instead that there's an implied ; (at the newline) after b. Thus, c; is left as a standalone expression statement.

Similarly:

```
var a = 42, b = "foo";

a
b   // "foo"
```

That's still a valid program without error, because expression statements also accept ASI.

There's certain places where ASI is helpful, like for instance:

```
var a = 42;

do {
    // ..
} while (a) // <-- ; expected here!
a;
```

The grammar requires a ; after a do..while loop, but not after while or for loops. But most developers don't remember that! So, ASI helpfully steps in and inserts one.

As we said earlier in the chapter, statement blocks do not require ; termination, so ASI isn't necessary:

```
var a = 42;

while (a) {
    // ..
} // <-- no ; expected here
a;
```

The other major case where ASI kicks in is with the break, con tinue, return, and (ES6) yield keywords:

```
function foo(a) {
    if (!a) return
    a *= 2;
```

```
    // ..
}
```

The `return` statement doesn't carry across the newline to the a `*= 2` expression, as ASI assumes the `;` terminating the `return` statement. Of course, `return` statements *can* easily break across multiple lines, just not when there's nothing after `return` but the newline/line break:

```
function foo(a) {
    return (
        a * 2 + 3 / 12
    );
}
```

Identical reasoning applies to `break`, `continue`, and `yield`.

Error Correction

One of the most hotly contested *religious wars* in the JS community (besides tabs versus spaces) is whether to rely heavily/exclusively on ASI or not.

Most, but not all, semicolons are optional, but the two `;`s in the `for ( .. ) ..` loop header are required.

On the pro side of this debate, many developers believe that ASI is a useful mechanism that allows them to write more terse (and more "beautiful") code by omitting all but the strictly required `;`s (which are very few). It is often asserted that ASI makes many `;`s optional, so a correctly written program *without them* is no different than a correctly written program *with them*.

On the con side of the debate, many other developers will assert that there are *too many* places that can be accidental gotchas, especially for newer, less experienced developers, where unintended `;`s being magically inserted change the meaning. Similarly, some developers will argue that if they omit a semicolon, it's a flat-out mistake, and they want their tools (linters, etc.) to catch it before the JS engine *corrects* the mistake under the covers.

Let me just share my perspective. A strict reading of the spec implies that ASI is an "error correction" routine. What kind of error, you may ask? Specifically, a *parser error*. In other words, in an attempt to have the parser fail less, ASI lets it be more tolerant.

But tolerant of what? In my view, the only way a parser error occurs is if it's given an incorrect/errored program to parse. So, while ASI is strictly correcting parser errors, the only way it can get such errors is if there were first program authoring errors—omitting semicolons where the grammar rules require them.

So, to put it more bluntly, when I hear someone claim that they want to omit "optional semicolons," my brain translates that claim to "I want to write the most parser-broken program I can that will still work."

I find that to be a ludicrous position to take and the arguments of saving keystrokes and having more "beautiful code" to be weak at best.

Furthermore, I don't agree that this is the same thing as the spaces versus tabs debate—that it's purely cosmetic—but rather I believe it's a fundamental question of writing code that adheres to grammar requirements versus code that relies on grammar exceptions to just barely skate through.

Another way of looking at it is that relying on ASI is essentially considering newlines to be significant "whitespace." Other languages like Python have true significant whitespace. But is it really appropriate to think of JavaScript as having significant newlines as it stands today?

My take: use semicolons wherever you know they are "required," and limit your assumptions about ASI to a minimum.

But don't just take my word for it. Back in 2012, Brendan Eich, the creator of JavaScript, said the following (*http://brendaneich.com/2012/04/the-infernal-semicolon/*):

> The moral of this story: ASI is (formally speaking) a syntactic error correction procedure. If you start to code as if it were a universal significant-newline rule, you will get into trouble....I wish I had made newlines more significant in JS back in those ten days in May, 1995....Be careful not to use ASI as if it gave JS significant newlines.

Errors

Not only does JavaScript have different *subtypes* of errors (TypeError, ReferenceError, SyntaxError, etc.), but also the grammar defines certain errors to be enforced at compile time, as compared to all other errors that happen during runtime.

In particular, there have long been a number of specific conditions that should be caught and reported as "early errors" (during compilation). Any straight-up syntax error is an early error (e.g., a = ,), but also the grammar defines things that are syntactically valid but disallowed nonetheless.

Since execution of your code has not begun yet, these errors are not catchable with `try..catch`; instead, they will just fail the parsing/compilation of your program.

 There's no requirement in the spec about exactly how browsers (and developer tools) should report errors. So you may see variations across browsers in the following error examples, in the specific subtype of error that is reported or what the included error message text will be.

One simple example is with syntax inside a regular expression literal. There's nothing wrong with the JS syntax here, but the invalid regex will throw an early error:

```
var a = /+foo/;     // Error!
```

The target of an assignment must be an identifier (or an ES6 destructuring expression that produces one or more identifiers), so a value like 42 in that position is illegal and can be reported right away:

```
var a;
42 = a;     // Error!
```

ES5's `strict` mode defines even more early errors. For example, in `strict` mode, function parameter names cannot be duplicated:

```
function foo(a,b,a) { }              // just fine

function bar(a,b,a) { "use strict"; }   // Error!
```

Another `strict` mode early error is an object literal having more than one property of the same name:

```
(function(){
    "use strict";

    var a = {
```

```
            b: 42,
            b: 43
    };              // Error!
})();
```

 Semantically speaking, such errors aren't technically *syntax* errors but more *grammar* errors—the above snippets are syntactically valid. But since there is no `GrammarError` type, some browsers use `SyntaxError` instead.

Using Variables Too Early

ES6 defines a (frankly confusingly named) new concept called the TDZ ("Temporal Dead Zone").

The TDZ refers to places in code where a variable reference cannot yet be made, because it hasn't reached its required initialization.

The most clear example of this is with ES6 `let` block-scoping:

```
{
    a = 2;      // ReferenceError!
    let a;
}
```

The assigment `a = 2` is accessing the `a` variable (which is indeed block-scoped to the `{ .. }` block) before it's been initialized by the `let a` declaration, so it's in the TDZ for `a` and throws an error.

Interestingly, while `typeof` has an exception to be safe for undeclared variables (see Chapter 1), no such safety exception is made for TDZ references:

```
{
    typeof a;   // undefined
    typeof b;   // ReferenceError! (TDZ)
    let b;
}
```

Function Arguments

Another example of a TDZ violation can be seen with ES6 default parameter values (see the *ES6 & Beyond* title in this series):

```
var b = 3;

function foo( a = 42, b = a + b + 5 ) {
```

```
        // ..
    }
```

The b reference in the assignment would happen in the TDZ for the parameter b (not pull in the outer b reference), so it will throw an error. However, the a is fine since by that time it's past the TDZ for parameter a.

When using ES6's default parameter values, the default value is applied to the parameter if you either omit an argument, or you pass an undefined value in its place:

```
function foo( a = 42, b = a + 1 ) {
    console.log( a, b );
}

foo();                  // 42 43
foo( undefined );       // 42 43
foo( 5 );               // 5 6
foo( void 0, 7 );       // 42 7
foo( null );            // null 1
```

null is coerced to a 0 value in the a + 1 expression. See Chapter 4 for more info.

From the ES6 default parameter values perspective, there's no difference between omitting an argument and passing an undefined value. However, there is a way to detect the difference in some cases:

```
function foo( a = 42, b = a + 1 ) {
    console.log(
        arguments.length, a, b,
        arguments[0], arguments[1]
    );
}

foo();                   // 0 42 43 undefined undefined
foo( 10 );               // 1 10 11 10 undefined
foo( 10, undefined );    // 2 10 11 10 undefined
foo( 10, null );         // 2 10 null 10 null
```

Even though the default parameter values are applied to the a and b parameters, if no arguments were passed in those slots, the arguments array will not have entries.

Conversely, if you pass an undefined argument explicitly, an entry will exist in the arguments array for that argument, but it will be undefined and not (necessarily) the same as the default value that was applied to the named parameter for that same slot.

While ES6 default parameter values can create divergence between the arguments array slot and the corresponding named parameter variable, this same disjointedness can also occur in tricky ways in ES5:

```
function foo(a) {
    a = 42;
    console.log( arguments[0] );
}

foo( 2 );    // 42 (linked)
foo();       // undefined (not linked)
```

If you pass an argument, the arguments slot and the named parameter are linked to always have the same value. If you omit the argument, no such linkage occurs.

But in strict mode, the linkage doesn't exist regardless:

```
function foo(a) {
    "use strict";
    a = 42;
    console.log( arguments[0] );
}

foo( 2 );    // 2 (not linked)
foo();       // undefined (not linked)
```

It's almost certainly a bad idea to ever rely on any such linkage, and in fact the linkage itself is a leaky abstraction that's exposing an underlying implementation detail of the engine, rather than a properly designed feature.

Use of the arguments array has been deprecated (especially in favor of ES6 ... rest parameters—see the *ES6 & Beyond* title in this series), but that doesn't mean that it's all bad.

Prior to ES6, arguments is the only way to get an array of all passed arguments to pass along to other functions, which turns out to be quite useful. You can also mix named parameters with the arguments array and be safe, as long as you follow one simple rule: *never refer to a named parameter and its corresponding arguments slot at the same time.* If you avoid that bad practice, you'll never expose the leaky linkage behavior:

```
function foo(a) {
    console.log( a + arguments[1] ); // safe!
}

foo( 10, 32 );  // 42
```

try..finally

You're probably familiar with how the `try..catch` block works. But have you ever stopped to consider the `finally` clause that can be paired with it? In fact, were you aware that `try` only requires either `catch` or `finally`, though both can be present if needed?

The code in the `finally` clause *always* runs (no matter what), and it always runs right after the `try` (and `catch` if present) finish, before any other code runs. In one sense, you can kind of think of the code in a `finally` clause as being in a callback function that will always be called regardless of how the rest of the block behaves.

So what happens if there's a `return` statement inside a `try` clause? It obviously will return a value, right? But does the calling code that receives that value run before or after the `finally`?

```
function foo() {
        try {
                return 42;
        }
        finally {
                console.log( "Hello" );
        }

        console.log( "never runs" );
}

console.log( foo() );
// Hello
// 42
```

The `return 42` runs right away, which sets up the completion value from the `foo()` call. This action completes the `try` clause and the `finally` clause immediately runs next. Only then is the `foo()` function complete, so that its completion value is returned back for the `console.log(..)` statement to use.

The exact same behavior is true of a throw inside try:

```
function foo() {
        try {
                throw 42;
        }
        finally {
                console.log( "Hello" );
        }

        console.log( "never runs" );
}

console.log( foo() );
// Hello
// Uncaught Exception: 42
```

Now, if an exception is thrown (accidentally or intentionally) inside a finally clause, it will override as the primary completion of that function. If a previous return in the try block had set a completion value for the function, that value will be abandoned:

```
function foo() {
        try {
                return 42;
        }
        finally {
                throw "Oops!";
        }

        console.log( "never runs" );
}

console.log( foo() );
// Uncaught Exception: Oops!
```

It shouldn't be surprising that other nonlinear control statements like continue and break exhibit similar behavior to return and throw:

```
for (var i=0; i<10; i++) {
        try {
                continue;
        }
        finally {
                console.log( i );
        }
}
// 0 1 2 3 4 5 6 7 8 9
```

The `console.log(i)` statement runs at the end of the loop iteration, which is caused by the `continue` statement. However, it still runs before the `i++` iteration update statement, which is why the values printed are `0..9` instead of `1..10`.

> ES6 adds a `yield` statement, in generators (see the *Async & Performance* title in this series) which in some ways can be seen as an intermediate `return` statement. However, unlike a `return`, a `yield` isn't complete until the generator is resumed, which means a `try { .. yield .. }` has not completed. So an attached `finally` clause will not run right after the `yield` like it does with `return`.

A `return` inside a `finally` has the special ability to override a previous `return` from the `try` or `catch` clause, but only if `return` is explicitly called:

```
function foo() {
        try {
                return 42;
        }
        finally {
                // no `return ..` here, so no override
        }
}

function bar() {
        try {
                return 42;
        }
        finally {
                // override previous `return 42`
                return;
        }
}

function baz() {
        try {
                return 42;
        }
        finally {
                // override previous `return 42`
                return "Hello";
        }
}
```

```
foo();  // 42
bar();  // undefined
baz();  // Hello
```

Normally, the omission of `return` in a function is the same as `return;` or even `return undefined;`, but inside a `finally` block the omission of `return` does not act like an overriding `return unde fined;` it just lets the previous `return` stand.

In fact, we can really up the craziness if we combine `finally` with labeled `break` (see "Labels" on page 131):

```
function foo() {
        bar: {
                try {
                        return 42;
                }
                finally {
                        // break out of `bar` labeled block
                        break bar;
                }
        }

        console.log( "Crazy" );

        return "Hello";
}

console.log( foo() );
// Crazy
// Hello
```

But... don't do this. Seriously. Using a `finally` + labeled `break` to effectively cancel a `return` is doing your best to create the most confusing code possible. I'd wager no amount of comments will redeem this code.

switch

Let's briefly explore the `switch` statement, a sort-of syntactic shorthand for an `if..else if..else..` statement chain:

```
switch (a) {
        case 2:
                // do something
                break;
        case 42:
                // do another thing
```

```
                break;
        default:
                // fallback to here
}
```

As you can see, it evaluates a once, then matches the resulting value to each case expression (just simple value expressions here). If a match is found, execution will begin in that matched case, and will either go until a break is encountered or until the end of the switch block is found.

That much may not surprise you, but there are several quirks about switch you may not have noticed before.

First, the matching that occurs between the a expression and each case expression is identical to the === algorithm (see Chapter 4). Often times switches are used with absolute values in case statements, as shown above, so strict matching is appropriate.

However, you may wish to allow coercive equality (aka ==, see Chapter 4), and to do so you'll need to sort of "hack" the switch statement a bit:

```
var a = "42";

switch (true) {
        case a == 10:
                console.log( "10 or '10'" );
                break;
        case a == 42:
                console.log( "42 or '42'" );
                break;
        default:
                // never gets here
}
// 42 or '42'
```

This works because the case clause can have any expression (not just simple values), which means it will strictly match that expression's result to the test expression (true). Since a == 42 results in true here, the match is made.

Despite ==, the switch matching itself is still strict, between true and true here. If the case expression resulted in something that was truthy but not strictly true (see Chapter 4), it wouldn't work. This can bite you if you're for instance using a "logical operator" like ||
or && in your expression:

```
var a = "hello world";
var b = 10;

switch (true) {
        case (a || b == 10):
                // never gets here
                break;
        default:
                console.log( "Oops" );
}
// Oops
```

Since the result of (a || b == 10) is "hello world" and not true, the strict match fails. In this case, the fix is to force the expression explicitly to be a true or false, such as case !!(a || b == 10): (see Chapter 4).

Lastly, the default clause is optional, and it doesn't necessarily have to come at the end (although that's the strong convention). Even in the default clause, the same rules apply about encountering a break or not:

```
var a = 10;

switch (a) {
        case 1:
        case 2:
                // never gets here
        default:
                console.log( "default" );
        case 3:
                console.log( "3" );
                break;
        case 4:
                console.log( "4" );
}
// default
// 3
```

 As discussed previously about labeled breaks, the break inside a case clause can also be labeled.

The way this snippet processes is that it passes through all the case clause matching first, finds no match, then goes back up to the default clause and starts executing. Since there's no break there, it continues executing in the already skipped over `case` 3 block, before stopping once it hits that `break`.

While this sort of roundabout logic is clearly possible in JavaScript, there's almost no chance that it's going to make for reasonable or understandable code. Be very skeptical if you find yourself wanting to create such circular logic flow, and if you really do, make sure you include plenty of code comments to explain what you're up to!

Review

JavaScript grammar has plenty of nuance that we as developers should spend a little more time paying closer attention to than we typically do. A little bit of effort goes a long way to solidifying your deeper knowledge of the language.

Statements and expressions have analogs in English language—statements are like sentences and expressions are like phrases. Expressions can be pure/self-contained, or they can have side effects.

The JavaScript grammar layers semantic usage rules (aka context) on top of the pure syntax. For example, { } pairs used in various places in your program can mean statement blocks, `object` literals, (ES6) destructuring assignments, or (ES6) named function arguments.

JavaScript operators all have well-defined rules for precedence (which ones bind first before others) and associativity (how multiple operator expressions are implicitly grouped). Once you learn these rules, it's up to you to decide if precedence/associativity are *too implicit* for their own good, or if they will aid in writing shorter, clearer code.

ASI (Automatic Semicolon Insertion) is a parser-error-correction mechanism built into the JS engine, which allows it under certain circumstances to insert an assumed ; in places where it is required, was omitted, *and* where insertion fixes the parser error. The debate rages over whether this behavior implies that most ;s are optional (and can/should be omitted for cleaner code) or whether it means that omitting them is making mistakes that the JS engine merely cleans up for you.

JavaScript has several types of errors, but it's less known that it has two classifications for errors: "early" (compiler thrown, uncatchable) and "runtime" (`try..catch`able). All syntax errors are obviously early errors that stop the program before it runs, but there are others, too.

Function arguments have an interesting relationship to their formal declared named parameters. Specifically, the `arguments` array has a number of gotchas of leaky abstraction behavior if you're not careful. Avoid `arguments` if you can, but if you must use it, by all means avoid using the positional slot in `arguments` at the same time as using a named parameter for that same argument.

The `finally` clause attached to a `try` (or `try..catch`) offers some very interesting quirks in terms of execution processing order. Some of these quirks can be helpful, but it's possible to create lots of confusion, especially if combined with labeled blocks. As always, use `finally` to make code better and clearer, not more clever or confusing.

The `switch` offers some nice shorthand for `if..else if..` statements, but beware of many common simplifying assumptions about its behavior. There are several quirks that can trip you up if you're not careful, but there's also some neat hidden tricks that `switch` has up its sleeve!

Mixed Environment JavaScript

Beyond the core language mechanics we've fully explored in this book, there are several ways that your JS code can behave differently when it runs in the real world. If JS was executing purely inside an engine, it'd be entirely predictable based on nothing but the black-and-white of the spec. But JS pretty much always runs in the context of a hosting environment, which exposes your code to some degree of unpredictability.

For example, when your code runs alongside code from other sources, or when your code runs in different types of JS engines (not just browsers), there are some things that may behave differently.

We'll briefly explore some of these concerns.

Annex B (ECMAScript)

It's a little known fact that the official name of the language is ECMAScript (referring to the ECMA standards body that manages it). What then is "JavaScript"? JavaScript is the common tradename of the language, of course, but more appropriately, JavaScript is basically the browser implementation of the spec.

The official ECMAScript specification includes "Annex B," which discusses specific deviations from the official spec for the purposes of JS compatibility in browsers.

The proper way to consider these deviations is that they are only reliably present/valid if your code is running in a browser. If your code always runs in browsers, you won't see any observable difference. If not (like if it can run in node.js, Rhino, etc.), or you're not sure, tread carefully.

The main compatibility differences:

- Octal number literals are allowed, such as `0123` (decimal 83) in non-`strict` mode.

- `window.escape(..)` and `window.unescape(..)` allow you to escape or unescape strings with %-delimited hexadecimal escape sequences. For example: `window.escape( "?foo=97%&bar=3%" )` produces `"%3Ffoo%3D97%25%26bar%3D3%25"`.

- `String.prototype.substr` is quite similar to `String.prototype.substring`, except that instead of the second parameter being the ending index (noninclusive), the second parameter is the `length` (number of characters to include).

Web ECMAScript

The Web ECMAScript specification (*https://javascript.spec.whatwg.org*) covers the differences between the official ECMAScript specification and the current JavaScript implementations in browsers.

In other words, these items are "required" of browsers (to be compatible with each other) but are not (as of the time of writing) listed in the "Annex B" section of the official spec:

- `<!--` and `-->` are valid single-line comment delimiters.

- `String.prototype` additions for returning HTML-formatted strings: `anchor(..)`, `big(..)`, `blink(..)`, `bold(..)`, `fixed(..)`, `fontcolor(..)`, `fontsize(..)`, `italics(..)`, `link(..)`, `small(..)`, `strike(..)`, and `sub(..)`.

These are very rarely used in practice, and are generally discouraged in favor of other built-in DOM APIs or user-defined utilities.

- RegExp extensions: `RegExp.$1 .. RegExp.$9` (match groups) and `RegExp.lastMatch/RegExp["$&"]` (most recent match).

- `Function.prototype` additions: `Function.prototype.argu ments` (aliases internal `arguments` object) and `Function.caller` (aliases internal `arguments.caller`).

 `arguments` and thus `arguments.caller` are deprecated, so you should avoid using them if possible. That goes doubly so for these aliases—don't use them!

 Some other minor and rarely used deviations are not included in our list here. See the external "Annex B" and "Web ECMAScript" documents for more detailed information as needed.

Generally speaking, all these differences are rarely used, so the deviations from the specification are not significant concerns. Just be careful if you rely on any of them.

Host Objects

The well-covered rules for how variables behave in JS have exceptions to them when it comes to variables that are auto-defined, or otherwise created and provided to JS by the environment that hosts your code (browser, etc.)—so-called "host objects" (which include both built-in `objects` and `functions`).

For example:

```
var a = document.createElement( "div" );

typeof a;                         // "object"--as expected
Object.prototype.toString.call( a ); // "[object HTMLDivElement]"

a.tagName;                        // "DIV"
```

a is not just an `object`, but a special host object because it's a DOM element. It has a different internal `[[Class]]` value (`"HTMLDivEle ment"`) and comes with predefined (and often unchangeable) properties.

Another such quirk has already been covered, in the "Falsy Objects" section in Chapter 4: some objects can exist but when coerced to `boolean` they (confoundingly) will coerce to `false` instead of the expected `true`.

Other behavior variations with host objects to be aware of can include:

- Not having access to normal `object` built-ins like `toString()`
- Not being overwritable
- Having certain predefined read-only properties
- Having methods that cannot be `this`-overridden to other objects
- And more...

Host objects are critical to making our JS code work with its surrounding environment. But it's important to note when you're interacting with a host object and to be careful assuming its behaviors, as they will quite often not conform to regular JS `objects`.

One notable example of a host object that you probably interact with regularly is the `console` object and its various functions (`log(..)`, `error(..)`, etc.). The `console` object is provided by the hosting environment specifically so your code can interact with it for various development-related output tasks.

In browsers, `console` hooks up to the developer tools' console display, whereas in node.js and other server-side JS environments, `console` is generally connected to the standard-output (`stdout`) and standard-error (`stderr`) streams of the JavaScript environment system process.

Global DOM Variables

You're probably aware that declaring a variable in the global scope (with or without `var`) creates not only a global variable, but also its mirror: a property of the same name on the `global` object (`window` in the browser).

But what may be less common knowledge is that (because of legacy browser behavior) creating DOM elements with `id` attributes creates global variables of those same names. For example:

```
<div id="foo"></div>
```

And:

```
if (typeof foo == "undefined") {
    foo = 42;          // will never run
}

console.log( foo );  // HTML element
```

You're perhaps used to managing global variable tests (using `typeof` or `..` in `window` checks) under the assumption that only JS code creates such variables, but as you can see, the contents of your hosting HTML page can also create them, which can easily throw off your existence check logic if you're not careful.

This is yet one more reason why you should, if at all possible, avoid using global variables, and if you have to, use variables with unique names that won't likely collide. But you also need to make sure not to collide with the HTML content as well as any other code.

Native Prototypes

One of the most widely known and classic pieces of JavaScript *best practice* wisdom is: never extend native prototypes.

Whatever method or property name you come up with to add to `Array.prototype` that doesn't (yet) exist, if it's a useful addition, well-designed, and properly named, there's a strong chance it *could* eventually end up being added to the spec—in which case your extension is now in conflict.

Here's a real example that actually happened to me that illustrates this point well.

I was building an embeddable widget for other websites, and my widget relied on jQuery (though pretty much any framework would have suffered this gotcha). It worked on almost every site, but we ran across one where it was totally broken.

After almost a week of analysis/debugging, I found that the site in question had, buried deep in one of its legacy files, code that looked like this:

```
// Netscape 4 doesn't have Array.push
Array.prototype.push = function(item) {
    this[this.length-1] = item;
};
```

Aside from the crazy comment (who cares about Netscape 4 anymore!?), this looks reasonable, right?

The problem is, `Array.prototype.push` was added to the spec sometime subsequent to this Netscape 4 era coding, but what was added is not compatible with this code. The standard `push(..)` allows multiple items to be pushed at once. This hacked one ignores the subsequent items.

Basically all JS frameworks have code that relies on `push(..)` with multiple elements. In my case, it was code around the CSS selector engine that was completely busted. But there could conceivably be dozens of other places susceptible.

The developer who originally wrote that `push(..)` hack had the right instinct to call it `push`, but didn't foresee pushing multiple elements. They were certainly acting in good faith, but they created a landmine that didn't go off until almost 10 years later when I unwittingly came along.

There's multiple lessons to take away on all sides.

First, don't extend the natives unless you're absolutely sure your code is the only code that will ever run in that environment. If you can't say that 100%, then extending the natives is dangerous. You must weigh the risks.

Next, don't unconditionally define extensions (because you can overwrite natives accidentally). For this particular example, consider the following code:

```
if (!Array.prototype.push) {
    // Netscape 4 doesn't have Array.push
    Array.prototype.push = function(item) {
        this[this.length-1] = item;
    };
}
```

Here, the `if` statement guard would have only defined this hacked `push()` for JS environments where it didn't exist. In my case, that probably would have been OK. But even this approach is not without risk:

1. If the site's code (for some crazy reason!) was relying on a push(..) that ignored multiple items, that code would have been broken years ago when the standard push(..) was rolled out.

2. If any other library had come in and hacked in a push(..) ahead of this if guard, and it did so in an incompatible way, that would have broken the site at that time.

What that highlights is an interesting question that, frankly, doesn't get enough attention from JS developers: should you *ever* rely on native built-in behavior if your code is running in any environment where it's not the only code present?

The strict answer is no, but that's awfully impractical. Your code usually can't redefine its own private untouchable versions of all built-in behavior relied on. Even if you *could*, that's pretty wasteful.

So, should you feature-test for the built-in behavior as well as compliance-test that it does what you expect? And what if that test fails—should your code just refuse to run?

```
// don't trust Array.prototype.push
(function(){
    if (Array.prototype.push) {
        var a = [];
        a.push(1,2);
        if (a[0] === 1 && a[1] === 2) {
            // tests passed, safe to use!
            return;
        }
    }

    throw Error(
        "Array#push() is missing/broken!"
    );
})();
```

In theory, that sounds plausible, but it's also pretty impractical to design tests for every single built-in method.

So, what should we do? Should we *trust but verify* (feature- and compliance-test) everything? Should we just assume existence is compliance and let breakage (caused by others) bubble up as it will?

There's no great answer. The only fact that can be observed is that extending native prototypes is the only way these things bite you.

If you don't do it, and no one else does in the code in your application, you're safe. Otherwise, you should build in at least a little bit of skepticism, pessimism, and expectation of possible breakage.

Having a full set of unit/regression tests of your code that runs in all known environments is one way to surface some of these issues earlier, but it doesn't do anything to actually protect you from these conflicts.

Shims/Polyfills

It's usually said that the only safe place to extend a native is in an older (non-spec-compliant) environment, since that's unlikely to ever change—new browsers with new spec features replace older browsers rather than amending them.

If you could see into the future, and know for sure what a future standard was going to be, like for `Array.prototype.foobar`, it'd be totally safe to make your own compatible version of it to use now, right?

```
if (!Array.prototype.foobar) {
    // silly, silly
    Array.prototype.foobar = function() {
        this.push( "foo", "bar" );
    };
}
```

If there's already a spec for `Array.prototype.foobar`, and the specified behavior is equal to this logic, you're pretty safe in defining such a snippet, and in that case it's generally called a "polyfill" (or "shim").

Such code is very useful to include in your code base to "patch" older browser environments that aren't updated to the newest specs. Using polyfills is a great way to create predictable code across all your supported environments.

ES5-Shim (*https://github.com/es-shims/es5-shim*) is a comprehensive collection of shims/polyfills for bringing a project up to ES5 baseline, and similarly, ES6-Shim (*https://github.com/es-shims/ es6-shim*) provides shims for new APIs added as of ES6. While APIs can be shimmed/polyfilled, new syntax generally cannot. To bridge the syntactic divide, you'll want to also use an ES6-to-ES5 transpiler like Traceur (*https://github.com/ google/traceur-compiler/wiki/GettingStarted*).

If there's likely a coming standard, and most discussions agree what it's going to be called and how it will operate, creating the ahead-of-time polyfill for future-facing standards compliance is called "prollyfill" (probably fill).

The real catch is if some new standard behavior can't be (fully) polyfilled/prollyfilled.

There's debate in the community if a partial polyfill for the common cases is acceptable (documenting the parts that cannot be polyfilled), or if a polyfill should be avoided if it can't be 100% compliant to the spec.

Many developers at least accept some common partial polyfills (like for instance `Object.create(..)`), because the parts that aren't covered are not parts they intend to use anyway.

Some developers believe that the `if` guard around a polyfill/shim should include some form of conformance test, replacing the existing method either if it's absent or fails the tests. This extra layer of compliance testing is sometimes used to distinguish a "shim" (compliance tested) from a "polyfill" (existence checked).

The only absolute takeaway is that there is no absolute *right* answer here. Extending natives, even when done "safely" in older environments, is not 100% safe. The same goes for relying upon (possibly extended) natives in the presence of others' code.

Either should always be done with caution, defensive code, and lots of obvious documentation about the risks.

<script>s

Most browser-viewed websites/applications have more than one file that contains their code, and it's common to have a few or several `<script src=..></script>` elements in the page that load these files separately, and even a few inline-code `<script> .. </script>` elements as well.

But do these separate files/code snippets constitute separate programs or are they collectively one JS program?

The (perhaps surprising) reality is they act more like independent JS programs in most, but not all, respects.

The one thing they *share* is the single `global` object (`window` in the browser), which means multiple files can append their code to that shared namespace and they can all interact.

So, if one `script` element defines a global function `foo()`, when a second `script` later runs, it can access and call `foo()` just as if it had defined the function itself.

But global variable scope *hoisting* (see the *Scope & Closures* title of this series) does not occur across these boundaries, so the following code would not work (because `foo()`'s declaration isn't yet declared), regardless of if they are (as shown) inline `<script> .. </script>` elements or externally loaded `<script src=..></script>` files:

```
<script>foo();</script>

<script>
  function foo() { .. }
</script>
```

But either of these *would* work instead:

```
<script>
  foo();
  function foo() { .. }
</script>
```

Or:

```
<script>
  function foo() { .. }
</script>

<script>foo();</script>
```

Also, if an error occurs in a `script` element (inline or external), as a separate standalone JS program it will fail and stop, but any subsequent `scripts` will run (still with the shared `global`) unimpeded.

You can create `script` elements dynamically from your code, and inject them into the DOM of the page, and the code in them will behave basically as if loaded normally in a separate file:

```
var greeting = "Hello World";

var el = document.createElement( "script" );

el.text = "function foo(){ alert( greeting );\
 } setTimeout( foo, 1000 );";

document.body.appendChild( el );
```

 Of course, if you tried the above snippet but set `el.src` to some file URL instead of setting `el.text` to the code contents, you'd be dynamically creating an externally loaded `<script src=..></script>` element.

One difference between code in an inline code block and that same code in an external file is that in the inline code block, the sequence of characters `</script>` cannot appear together, as (regardless of where it appears) it would be interpreted as the end of the code block. So, beware of code like:

```
<script>
  var code = "<script>alert( 'Hello World' )</script>";
</script>
```

It looks harmless, but the `</script>` appearing inside the `string` literal will terminate the script block abnormally, causing an error. The most common workaround is:

```
"</sc" + "ript>";
```

Also, beware that code inside an external file will be interpreted in the character set (UTF-8, ISO-8859-8, etc.) the file is served with (or the default), but that same code in an inline `script` element in your HTML page will be interpreted by the character set of the page (or its default).

The charset attribute will not work on inline script elements.

Another deprecated practice with inline `script` elements is including HTML-style or X(HT)ML-style comments around inline code, like:

```
<script>
<!--
alert( "Hello" );
//-->
</script>

<script>
<!--//--><![CDATA[//><!--
alert( "World" );
//--><!]]>
</script>
```

Both of these are totally unnecessary now, so if you're still doing that, stop it!

 Both `<!--` and `-->` (HTML-style comments) are actually specified as valid single-line comment delimiters (`var x = 2; <!-- valid comment` and `--> another valid line comment`) in JavaScript (see the "Web ECMAScript" section earlier), purely because of this old technique. But never use them.

Reserved Words

The ES5 spec defines a set of "reserved words" in Section 7.6.1 that cannot be used as standalone variable names. Technically, there are four categories: "keywords," "future reserved words," the `null` literal, and the `true`/`false` boolean literals.

Keywords are the obvious ones like `function` and `switch`. Future reserved words include things like `enum`, though many of the rest of them (`class`, `extends`, etc.) are all now actually used by ES6; there are other `strict` mode-only reserved words like `interface`.

StackOverflow user "art4theSould" creatively worked all these reserved words into a fun little poem (*http://stackoverflow.com/ques tions/26255/reserved-keywords-in-javascript/12114140#12114140*):

Let this long package float,
Goto private class if short.
While protected with debugger case,
Continue volatile interface.
Instanceof super synchronized throw,
Extends final export throws.

Try import double enum?
- False, boolean, abstract function,
Implements typeof transient break!
Void static, default do,
Switch int native new.
Else, delete null public var
In return for const, true, char
…Finally catch byte.

This poem includes words that were reserved in ES3 (byte, long, etc.) that are no longer reserved as of ES5.

Prior to ES5, the reserved words also could not be property names or keys in object literals, but that restriction no longer exists.

So, this is not allowed:

```
var import = "42";
```

But this is allowed:

```
var obj = { import: "42" };
console.log( obj.import );
```

You should be aware though that some older browser versions (mainly older IE) weren't completely consistent on applying these rules, so there are places where using reserved words in object property name locations can still cause issues. Carefully test all supported browser environments.

Implementation Limits

The JavaScript spec does not place arbitrary limits on things such as the number of arguments to a function or the length of a string literal, but these limits exist nonetheless, because of implementation details in different engines.

For example:

```
function addAll() {
        var sum = 0;
        for (var i=0; i < arguments.length; i++) {
                sum += arguments[i];
        }
        return sum;
}

var nums = [];
for (var i=1; i < 100000; i++) {
        nums.push(i);
}

addAll( 2, 4, 6 );          // 12
addAll.apply( null, nums ); // should be: 499950000
```

In some JS engines, you'll get the correct 499950000 answer, but in others (like Safari 6.x), you'll get the error "RangeError: Maximum call stack size exceeded."

Examples of other limits known to exist:

- Maximum number of characters allowed in a string literal (not just a string value)
- Size (bytes) of data that can be sent in arguments to a function call (aka stack size)
- Number of parameters in a function declaration
- Maximum depth of nonoptimized call stack (i.e., with recursion): how long a chain of function calls from one to the other can be
- Number of seconds a JS program can run continuously blocking the browser
- Maximum length allowed for a variable name

It's not very common at all to run into these limits, but you should be aware that limits can and do exist, and importantly that they vary between engines.

Review

We know and can rely upon the fact that the JS language itself has one standard and is predictably implemented by all the modern browsers/engines. This is a very good thing!

But JavaScript rarely runs in isolation. It runs in an environment mixed in with code from third-party libraries, and sometimes it even runs in engines/environments that differ from those found in browsers.

Paying close attention to these issues improves the reliability and robustness of your code.

Acknowledgments

I have many people to thank for making this book title and the overall series happen.

Firstly, I must thank my wife Christen Simpson, and my two kids Ethan and Emily, for putting up with Dad always pecking away at the computer. Even when not writing books, my obsession with JavaScript glues my eyes to the screen far more than it should. That time I borrow from my family is the reason these books can so deeply and completely explain JavaScript to you, the reader. I owe my family everything.

I'd like to thank my editors at O'Reilly, namely Simon St.Laurent and Brian MacDonald, as well as the rest of the editorial and marketing staff. They are fantastic to work with, and have been especially accommodating during this experiment into open source book writing, editing, and production.

Thank you to the many folks who have participated in making this series better by providing editorial suggestions and corrections, including Shelley Powers, Tim Ferro, Evan Borden, Forrest L Norvell, Jennifer Davis, Jesse Harlin, and many others. A big thank you to David Walsh for writing the Foreword for this title.

Thank you to the countless folks in the community, including members of the TC39 committee, who have shared so much knowledge with the rest of us, and especially tolerated my incessant questions and explorations with patience and detail. John-David Dalton, Juriy "kangax" Zaytsev, Mathias Bynens, Rick Waldron, Axel Rauschmayer, Nicholas Zakas, Angus Croll, Jordan Harband, Reginald Braithwaite, Dave Herman, Brendan Eich, Allen Wirfs-Brock, Bradley Meck, Domenic Denicola, David Walsh, Tim Disney, Kris Kowal, Peter van der Zee, Andrea Giammarchi, Kit Cambridge, and so many others, I can't even scratch the surface.

Since the *You Don't Know JS* series was born on Kickstarter, I also wish to thank all my (nearly) 500 generous backers, without whom this series could not have happened:

Jan Szpila, nokiko, Murali Krishnamoorthy, Ryan Joy, Craig Patchett, pdqtrader, Dale Fukami, ray hatfield, R0drigo Perez [Mx], Dan Petitt, Jack Franklin, Andrew Berry, Brian Grinstead, Rob Sutherland, Sergi Meseguer, Phillip Gourley, Mark Watson, Jeff Carouth, Alfredo Sumaran, Martin Sachse, Marcio Barrios, Dan, AimelyneM, Matt Sullivan, Delnatte Pierre-Antoine, Jake Smith, Eugen Tudorancea, Iris, David Trinh, simonstl, Ray Daly, Uros Gruber, Justin Myers, Shai Zonis, Mom & Dad, Devin Clark, Dennis Palmer, Brian Panahi Johnson, Josh Marshall, Marshall, Dennis Kerr, Matt Steele, Erik Slagter, Sacah, Justin Rainbow, Christian Nilsson, Delapouite, D.Pereira, Nicolas Hoizey, George V. Reilly, Dan Reeves, Bruno Laturner, Chad Jennings, Shane King, Jeremiah Lee Cohick, od3n, Stan Yamane, Marko Vucinic, Jim B, Stephen Collins, Ægir Þorsteinsson, Eric Pederson, Owain, Nathan Smith, Jeanetteurphy, Alexandre ELISÉ, Chris Peterson, Rik Watson, Luke Matthews, Justin Lowery, Morten Nielsen, Vernon Kesner, Chetan Shenoy, Paul Tregoing, Marc Grabanski, Dion Almaer, Andrew Sullivan, Keith Elsass, Tom Burke, Brian Ashenfelter, David Stuart, Karl Swedberg, Graeme, Brandon Hays, John Christopher, Gior, manoj reddy, Chad Smith, Jared Harbour, Minoru TODA, Chris Wigley, Daniel Mee, Mike, Handyface, Alex Jahraus, Carl Furrow, Rob Foulkrod, Max Shishkin, Leigh Penny Jr., Robert Ferguson, Mike van Hoenselaar, Hasse Schougaard, rajan venkataguru, Jeff Adams, Trae Robbins, Rolf Langenhuijzen, Jorge Antunes, Alex Koloskov, Hugh Greenish, Tim Jones, Jose Ochoa, Michael Brennan-White, Naga Harish Muvva, Barkóczi Dávid, Kitt Hodsden, Paul McGraw, Sascha Goldhofer, Andrew Metcalf, Markus Krogh, Michael Mathews, Matt Jared, Juanfran, Georgie Kirschner, Kenny Lee, Ted Zhang, Amit Pahwa, Inbal Sinai, Dan Raine, Schabse Laks, Michael Tervoort, Alexandre Abreu, Alan Joseph Williams, NicolasD, Cindy Wong, Reg Braithwaite, LocalPCGuy, Jon Friskics, Chris Merriman, John Pena, Jacob Katz, Sue Lockwood, Magnus Johansson, Jeremy Crapsey, Grzegorz Pawłowski, nico nuzzaci, Christine Wilks, Hans Bergren, charles montgomery, Ariel בר-לבב Fogel, Ivan Kolev, Daniel Campos, Hugh Wood, Christian Bradford, Frédéric Harper, Ionuţ Dan Popa, Jeff Trimble,

Rupert Wood, Trey Carrico, Pancho Lopez, Joël kuijten, Tom A Marra, Jeff Jewiss, Jacob Rios, Paolo Di Stefano, Soledad Penades, Chris Gerber, Andrey Dolganov, Wil Moore III, Thomas Martineau, Kareem, Ben Thouret, Udi Nir, Morgan Laupies, jory carson-burson, Nathan L Smith, Eric Damon Walters, Derry Lozano-Hoyland, Geoffrey Wiseman, mkeehner, KatieK, Scott MacFarlane, Brian LaShomb, Adrien Mas, christopher ross, Ian Littman, Dan Atkinson, Elliot Jobe, Nick Dozier, Peter Wooley, John Hoover, dan, Martin A. Jackson, Héctor Fernando Hurtado, andy ennamorato, Paul Seltmann, Melissa Gore, Dave Pollard, Jack Smith, Philip Da Silva, Guy Israeli, @megalithic, Damian Crawford, Felix Gliesche, April Carter Grant, Heidi, jim tierney, Andrea Giammarchi, Nico Vignola, Don Jones, Chris Hartjes, Alex Howes, john gibbon, David J. Groom, BBox, Yu *Dilys* Sun, Nate Steiner, Brandon Satrom, Brian Wyant, Wesley Hales, Ian Pouncey, Timothy Kevin Oxley, George Terezakis, sanjay raj, Jordan Harband, Marko McLion, Wolfgang Kaufmann, Pascal Peuckert, Dave Nugent, Markus Liebelt, Welling Guzman, Nick Cooley, Daniel Mesquita, Robert Syvarth, Chris Coyier, Rémy Bach, Adam Dougal, Alistair Duggin, David Loidolt, Ed Richer, Brian Chenault, GoldFire Studios, Carles Andrés, Carlos Cabo, Yuya Saito, roberto ricardo, Barnett Klane, Mike Moore, Kevin Marx, Justin Love, Joe Taylor, Paul Dijou, Michael Kohler, Rob Cassie, Mike Tierney, Cody Leroy Lindley, tofuji, Shimon Schwartz, Raymond, Luc De Brouwer, David Hayes, Rhys Brett-Bowen, Dmitry, Aziz Khoury, Dean, Scott Tolinski - Level Up, Clement Boirie, Djordje Lukic, Anton Kotenko, Rafael Corral, Philip Hurwitz, Jonathan Pidgeon, Jason Campbell, Joseph C., SwiftOne, Jan Hohner, Derick Bailey, getify, Daniel Cousineau, Chris Charlton, Eric Turner, David Turner, Joël Galeran, Dharma Vagabond, adam, Dirk van Bergen, dave ♥♫★ furf, Vedran Zakanj, Ryan McAllen, Natalie Patrice Tucker, Eric J. Bivona, Adam Spooner, Aaron Cavano, Kelly Packer, Eric J, Martin Drenovac, Emilis, Michael Pelikan, Scott F. Walter, Josh Freeman, Brandon Hudgeons, vijay chennupati, Bill Glennon, Robin R., Troy Forster, otaku_coder, Brad, Scott, Frederick Ostrander, Adam Brill, Seb Flippence, Michael Anderson, Jacob, Adam Randlett, Standard, Joshua Clanton, Sebastian Kouba, Chris Deck, SwordFire, Hannes Papenberg, Richard Woeber, hnzz, Rob Crowther, Jedidiah Broadbent, Sergey Chernyshev, Jay-Ar Jamon, Ben Combee, luciano bonachela, Mark Tomlinson, Kit Cambridge, Michael Melgares, Jacob Adams, Adrian Bruinhout, Bev Wieber, Scott Puleo, Thomas Herzog, April Leone, Daniel Mizieliński, Kees van Ginkel, Jon Abrams, Erwin Heiser, Avi Laviad, David newell, Jean-Francois Turcot, Niko Roberts, Erik Dana, Charles Neill, Aaron Holmes, Grzegorz Ziółkowski, Nathan Youngman, Timothy, Jacob Mather, Michael Allan, Mohit Seth, Ryan Ewing, Benjamin Van Treese, Marcelo Santos, Denis Wolf, Phil Keys, Chris Yung, Timo Tijhof,

Martin Lekvall, Agendine, Greg Whitworth, Helen Humphrey, Dougal Campbell, Johannes Harth, Bruno Girin, Brian Hough, Darren Newton, Craig McPheat, Olivier Tille, Dennis Roethig, Mathias Bynens, Brendan Stromberger, sundeep, John Meyer, Ron Male, John F Croston III, gigante, Carl Bergenhem, B.J. May, Rebekah Tyler, Ted Foxberry, Jordan Reese, Terry Suitor, afeliz, Tom Kiefer, Darragh Duffy, Kevin Vanderbeken, Andy Pearson, Simon Mac Donald, Abid Din, Chris Joel, Tomas Theunissen, David Dick, Paul Grock, Brandon Wood, John Weis, dgrebb, Nick Jenkins, Chuck Lane, Johnny Megahan, marzsman, Tatu Tamminen, Geoffrey Knauth, Alexander Tarmolov, Jeremy Tymes, Chad Auld, Sean Parmelee, Rob Staenke, Dan Bender, Yannick derwa, Joshua Jones, Geert Plaisier, Tom LeZotte, Christen Simpson, Stefan Bruvik, Justin Falcone, Carlos Santana, Michael Weiss, Pablo Villoslada, Peter deHaan, Dimitris Iliopoulos, seyDoggy, Adam Jordens, Noah Kantrowitz, Amol M, Matthew Winnard, Dirk Ginader, Phinam Bui, David Rapson, Andrew Baxter, Florian Bougel, Michael George, Alban Escalier, Daniel Sellers, Sasha Rudan, John Green, Robert Kowalski, David I. Teixeira (@ditma, Charles Carpenter, Justin Yost, Sam S, Denis Ciccale, Kevin Sheurs, Yannick Croissant, Pau Fracés, Stephen McGowan, Shawn Searcy, Chris Ruppel, Kevin Lamping, Jessica Campbell, Christopher Schmitt, Sablons, Jonathan Reisdorf, Bunni Gek, Teddy Huff, Michael Mullany, Michael Fürstenberg, Carl Henderson, Rick Yoesting, Scott Nichols, Hernán Ciudad, Andrew Maier, Mike Stapp, Jesse Shawl, Sérgio Lopes, jsulak, Shawn Price, Joel Clermont, Chris Ridmann, Sean Timm, Jason Finch, Aiden Montgomery, Elijah Manor, Derek Gathright, Jesse Harlin, Dillon Curry, Courtney Myers, Diego Cadenas, Arne de Bree, João Paulo Dubas, James Taylor, Philipp Kraeutli, Mihai Păun, Sam Gharegozlou, joshjs, Matt Murchison, Eric Windham, Timo Behrmann, Andrew Hall, joshua price, Théophile Villard

This series is being written in open source, including editing and production. We owe GitHub a debt of gratitude for making that sort of thing possible for the community!

Thank you again to all the countless folks I didn't name but who I nonetheless owe thanks. May this series be "owned" by all of us and serve to contribute to increasing awareness and understanding of the JavaScript language, to the benefit of all current and future community contributors.

About the Author

Kyle Simpson is an Open Web Evangelist from Austin, TX. He's passionate about JavaScript, HTML5, real-time/peer-to-peer communications, and web performance. Otherwise, he's probably bored by it. Kyle is an author, workshop trainer, tech speaker, and avid OSS community member.

Colophon

The cover font for *Types & Grammar* is Interstate. The text font is Adobe Minion Pro; the heading font is Adobe Myriad Condensed; and the code font is Dalton Maag's Ubuntu Mono.

Have it your way.

Get even more for your money.

Join the O'Reilly Community, and register the O'Reilly books you own. It's free, and you'll get:

- $4.99 ebook upgrade offer
- 40% upgrade offer on O'Reilly print books
- Membership discounts on books and events
- Free lifetime updates to ebooks and videos
- Multiple ebook formats, DRM FREE
- Participation in the O'Reilly community
- Newsletters
- Account management
- 100% Satisfaction Guarantee

Signing up is easy:

1. Go to: oreilly.com/go/register
2. Create an O'Reilly login.
3. Provide your address.
4. Register your books.

Note: English-language books only

To order books online:
oreilly.com/store

For questions about products or an order:
orders@oreilly.com

To sign up to get topic-specific email announcements and/or news about upcoming books, conferences, special offers, and new technologies:
elists@oreilly.com

For technical questions about book content:
booktech@oreilly.com

To submit new book proposals to our editors:
proposals@oreilly.com

O'Reilly books are available in multiple DRM-free ebook formats. For more information:
oreilly.com/ebooks

DISCARD

CPSIA information can be obtained at www.ICGtesting.com
Printed in the USA
BVOW08s2228290115

385646BV00005B/8/P